EASY **SINGER** STYLE™

quick and easy
window treatments

15 easy-sew projects that build skills, too

madlyn easley

Creative Publishing
international

contents

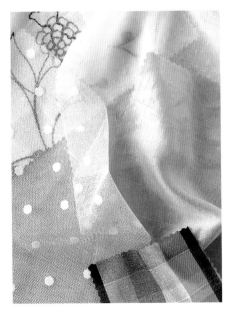

welcome to sewing!

Window fashions are among the easiest of all home furnishings to sew. They may be large, but they have simple shapes and one or only a few pieces, so they're not difficult to assemble. Besides, the fabric options are so lovely, it's hard to resist dreaming of ways to dress your windows. It's also satisfying to see the finished effect of your custom-made curtain or valance—so much nicer than ready-made pieces from a catalog and much less costly than hiring an interior designer to have them made for you.

In the first five chapters, you'll find essential information about fabric, window treatment design, equipment, measuring and planning, and basic sewing—everything you need to know in order to plan a project, buy your materials, and get started sewing. The following chapters feature a total of fifteen valance or curtain projects with complete step-by-step directions. You can make each project in any size you wish and from any fabric you adore.

The projects are arranged in order of complexity, so if you are new to sewing or unsure of your skills, try one of the simple designs on pages 41–61. If you're ready to take on a more detailed design, try the projects in Adding Pleats and Designer Details (pages 63–85). And when you're ready to really test your skills, turn to Working with Linings and Trims (pages 87–109). Whichever window treatment you choose, read through the steps before you begin so you understand the complete process—then measure, plan, and dive into the sewing fun.

Have fun! You can sew it!

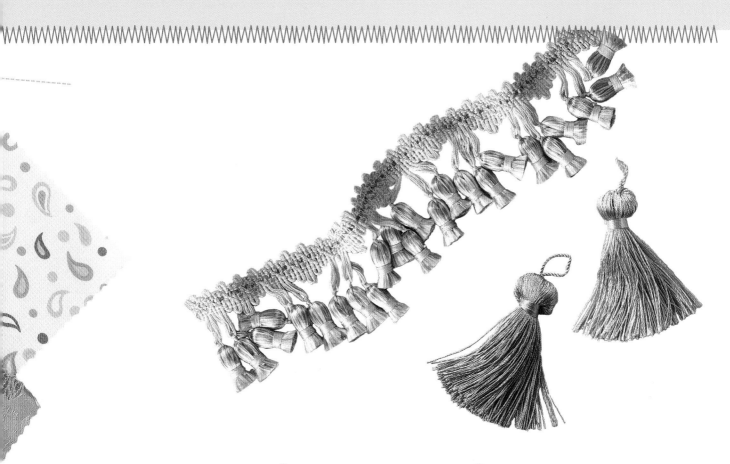

fabric facts

It's easy to fall in love with fabric. It's so beautiful! Printed patterns of every style and scale, intriguing textures, thousands of colors—the perfect material for your window treatment is waiting for you in a local shop or online. Before you purchase enough for a roomful of window treatments, buy a small amount so you can make sure you like the effect. Here is information that will help you make good choices.

Fabric and Style

As you look through the projects in this book, you'll see how fabric and window treatment design go hand in hand, but there are many possibilities. Every window treatment design can be made to look casual or dressy. You can decide when you choose the fabric. Curtains and valances are just flat pieces of fabric, sometimes gathered across the window, sometimes draped horizontally, and sometimes both. Every style can be made in plain muslin, graphic stripes or checks, a multicolored floral print, a luxurious embroidered satin, or dozens of other materials. Each fabric will change the look of the finished treatment. So, think about the treatment and the fabric at the same time.

Fabric Types

When choosing window treatment fabrics, you should consider two qualities: the weight of the fabric and whether it is patterned or plain. Are you looking for a fabric that's lightweight (perhaps sheer), medium weight, or heavy and dense? Do you want a solid, a pattern, or a texture? Home décor fabrics are the best choice. They are wide and often have a durable finish. Quilting fabrics and fashion fabrics work, too, as long as they are not slippery to handle. Choose whatever suits your decorating style.

Pattern

You can find fabrics that feature just about any kind of subject or style. There are floral and foliage patterns with a traditional or modern feel. You'll find birds, bees, butterflies, monkeys, lions, cats, and dogs. There are sporting and fashion prints, children's prints, hobby motifs, and classic motifs, such as bows, ribbons, and paisley patterns. There are graphic fabrics, too—dots, circles, squares, stripes, checks, and plaids of every imaginable type.

a few tips: Patterned fabrics often have a matte finish, but they may have natural sheen (like some silks) or a polished finish (like chintz). Patterned fabrics are easy to sew, but most patterns have to be matched at seams, so when you are planning your project, be sure you purchase enough fabric and cut it correctly.

Texture

Would you like a smooth fabric, like broadcloth or satin, or something slightly coarse, like linen or cotton canvas? Maybe an irregular weave with thick and thin threads combined, like dupioni or antique satin? Perhaps something velvety is what you have in mind? Or something with a loose, open weave, like casement cloth or lace?

a few tips: Textured fabrics vary greatly in weight—heavier ones may be difficult to sew or too bulky to gather or drape attractively. Textures may be single- or multicolored. Some woven patterns need to be matched at the seams.

Plain

Don't dismiss solid-color fabric—it can be very pretty. Every kind of fabric, from muslin and sheeting to chintz and silk, comes in solid colors. You might choose a solid-color accent, such as a border, for some window treatment designs.

a few tips: Fading and dirt are more apparent on plain fabric. If you are mixing plain and patterned fabric, purchase coordinating goods from a single manufacturer if you can—the weight and colors will be the same.

Lightweight

Lightweight fabrics include sheers, which produce an airy effect, and fine cottons and silks, which often look delicate or elegant. For sheers, you can choose among cottons and linens that are so loosely woven that they look like cheesecloth, voile (often a cotton-polyester blend), silk organza, or lace—sometimes with a border pattern. Many types of printed and plain cotton, linen, and silk are a little bit heavier but still very light.

a few tips: Lightweight fabrics tend to be translucent even if they're not truly sheer. Seams and hems will show as a "shadow" once the window treatments are on your window. Hem shadows can be attractive, but seams are likely to be distracting unless the treatment is full enough that the seams disappear in the folds.

glossary of terms

Here are some terms you might hear when discussing fabric.

Fiber: the plant, animal, or synthetic substance from which a fabric is woven.

Finish: a surface treatment applied to fabric after it is woven and printed.

Hand: the behavioral characteristics of a fabric; the way it "handles."

Opacity: the ability to block light.

Pattern: figures, motifs, and geometric or abstract designs printed on or woven into a fabric.

Repeat: the distance from one point in a specific motif to the same point in the nearest identical motif.

Shadow: the dense shapes that are visible when light shines through sheer or translucent window treatments.

Sheer: fabric you can see through.

Texture: the tactile surface of the fabric.

Translucency: the ability to transmit light.

Weave: the structure of a woven fabric.

Medium Weight

Medium-weight fabrics are the most common choices for window treatments. They're easy to handle and available in nearly endless variety. You'll find almost every pattern and solid color you can think of, usually in cotton, linen, silk, or a blend. Sheeting, ticking, chintz, brocade, dupioni, and taffeta are all medium-weight fabrics.

a few tips: Most medium-weight fabrics are a pleasure to work with. Some types (taffeta, for instance), may be too stiff to drape nicely, so test the effect if you are planning a tie-up, cloud, or balloon valance.

Heavyweight

Tapestry and velvet are two heavy-weight fabrics with great appeal. Thick, coarsely woven raw silk is another. These fabrics are best for flat window treatments or curtains that are hung on rings.

a few tips: It can be challenging to feed multiple layers of heavy fabric through a sewing machine. Although you can successfully sew some heavy-weight cotton and linen fabrics as curtains and valances, most thick fabrics simply look bulky and awkward unless the overall scale of the room and the treatment are grand.

Decorative Trims

Trims add a special touch to any window treatment, yet many people avoid them because they seem too fancy or too challenging to sew. There are lots of simple, informal trims that look wonderful, and unless your fabrics are very bulky, they're not difficult to sew on. Aside from tassels and buttons, there are two basic types of trims: those sewn to the surface of a project and those inserted into a seam.

a few tips: Choose trim that has the same care requirements as your fabric, or care for the fabric as the trim requires. Ribbon does not easily bend around curves, so don't use it on scalloped hemlines. Trim can be surprisingly costly and, depending on the treatment and the number of windows you're dressing, you may need many yards of it. Consider the cost of the trim when you choose your fabric—you might even want to select a less expensive fabric and dress it up with an extravagant trim.

Applied Trims

You can sew any trim that is finished on both edges onto the surface of your project. Ribbon, braid, gimp, rickrack, and some types of lace and eyelet are a few examples. You can also apply ruffles that are finished on both long edges and gathered with a heading. You can attach most fringes this way, too, but some types, which are designed to be inserted into a seam, come attached to an unattractive band.

Inserted Trims

Trim that is finished on only one edge should be inserted into a seam—usually between the lining and the face fabric. Insertion trims include dimensional trims that have a flange, such as some types of fringe and decorator cord or fabric-covered cord (both often called welting). Ruffles that are finished on only one edge are inserted into seams, too. So are some types of lace and eyelet. Rickrack inserted into a seam makes a cute edging.

choosing the right look

As you choose which project you'd like to make for your windows, you'll want to consider the basic treatment options—full curtains or a valance—and the specific design details. Before you make your final choice, and especially before you pass on any project you're unsure about, read this chapter. Each of the projects in this book can be easily adapted to hang inside or outside the window frame. Choosing the right proportion and the perfect hardware is simply part of your design process.

The Basic Window Treatment

Most of the projects in this book (all but three) have a channel called a rod pocket. The rod pocket is sewn at the top of the curtain to hold the curtain rod. It's really just a hem that is open at both ends. Sometimes this top hem is extra deep and actually extends above the rod pocket—and once installed, above the rod. This extension is called a heading.

The drawing at right shows a finished valance from the wrong side. You can see the rod pocket and the other basic construction elements. If you choose a project with a rod pocket, you can make it with or without the heading, as you wish. You just need to plan ahead, as described on page 28, and adapt the top allowance to suit your choice.

Rod-pocket curtains can be difficult to push open or pull closed. The fabric fits pretty tightly over the rod, so it has to be adjusted a bit at a time—which can be especially awkward if the rod is above your head! Rod-pocket construction is

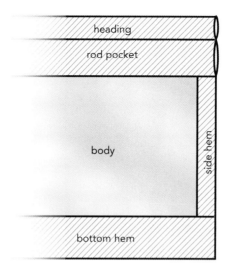

Wrong side of valance

best for valances, curtains that are always open, or curtains that you can adjust for privacy some other way. For example, you might hang a window shade or blinds in the window under the curtains. Or you might add tiebacks (page 83) or special hardware called holdbacks to hold the curtains open during the day and then release the curtains at night. Curtains that hang on rings are the easiest to open and close (page 53). If the rod surface is slippery, tab curtains (page 61) are often easy to adjust.

Inside and Outside Mounts

Most curtains and valances are installed on rods that hang in front of the window and span the side moldings and often some of the wall. This style of installation is called an **outside mount**. Or, the treatment can be installed on rods that fit within the window recess, leaving all the moldings visible. This option is called an **inside mount**. An inside mount is perfect for valances, café curtains, or any short curtain, but not as good for long curtains, which conceal the front of the windowsill and may look awkward. There are examples of both outside mounts and inside mounts in the projects.

If you choose an outside mount, you can select either a decorative curtain rod—with ornamental finials on each end—or a standard rod, which bends back to the wall at each end and is not visible when the treatment is hung. Select whichever type of rod you prefer for any of the rod-pocket projects in this book.

Rules of proportion

How do you know how wide a curtain should be or how much of the window a valance should cover? What is the right height for installing the rod? Is there a way to make your windows look wider or taller? The answers depend on whether you've chosen an inside mount or an outside mount. If you choose an outside mount for either curtains or a valance, you can make the window look taller by hanging the rod above it. If you are hanging curtains, you can make the window look wider by extending the rod on each side.

Here are general guides for proportion to consider as you decide how you'd like your treatment to fit into your décor. You'll consider these choices when you plan the exact dimensions later (pages 24–28).

Inside-mounted curtains must be wide enough to cover the window sash. The rod can be installed at the top of the recess, halfway up, or in line with any of the muntins (if the window has multiple panes of glass). Generally, you hem inside-mounted curtains at the level of the windowsill.

Outside-mounted curtains should be at least wide enough to span the window and cover the moldings—but you can make them as wide as you like. Generally, the rod length is slightly less than twice the window width, which allows you to open the curtains almost all the way off the window. Install the rod so the top of the curtain is level with the top of the molding.

For café curtains, install the rod halfway or three-quarters of the way up, or level with one of the upper muntins (if the window has multiple panes of glass). Short, outside-mounted curtains are usually hemmed at the bottom of the apron (the molding below the windowsill). If you want to make the window look taller, hang the rod for outside-mounted curtains or a valance above the molding.

Inside-mounted valances must be wide enough to cover the window sash. They are usually about one-quarter the length of the window or hemmed at one of the muntins (if the window has multiple panes of glass). If you shape the hemline, the shortest point should be at one of these levels.

Now that you know the rules, feel free to ignore them—a really short valance can be very cute, adding a frill to the top of your window.

Outside-mounted valances, used alone, should be wide enough to span the window and cover the moldings. If they're any wider, they'll look awkward—but if you decide to hang the valance over curtain panels, you should make it as wide as the curtains. Follow the same length suggestions for inside-mounted valances. If you opt for a short valance or choose to install the rod high above the window, just make sure the valance is long enough to cover the top window molding.

here's a hint!

You need to hold most rods at an angle to slide them onto their brackets. Be sure you leave enough space below the ceiling or below the top of the window recess to do this.

tools and supplies

It's a good idea to have on hand all the tools and supplies you'll need before you start. This way, you won't have to waste time looking for them when you'd rather be sewing! You sewing process will be more efficient and much more fun. Here is a simple guide to the gear you will need when measuring, pressing, marking, cutting, sewing, and hanging your curtains or valance.

Measuring Tools

You can easily find most of the measuring tools you'll need at a good art supply or sewing notions store. Look for lightweight metal and transparent acrylic measuring tools that are easy to handle. Steer clear of the heavy long rulers you find at the hardware store—they're designed for carpenters and will wrinkle fabric rather than glide across it. The projects instructions are explained with both the U.S. and metric systems of measurements. The measurements on inch and metric rulers are not consistent, so choose one method and stick with it.

Tape measures: Select a retractable metal tape measure at least 10' (3 m) long. The type that has a slider to lock the extended length is most useful. A standard flexible cloth or plastic tape measure is handy when making ties that wrap around a treatment.

Metal L-square: A large L-square with a 24" (61 cm) leg is essential when you are marking perpendicular lines.

Metal straightedge: A 4' (1.2 m) ruler is the ideal guide for marking long cutting lines.

Transparent acrylic rulers: Look for the type that is printed with a grid in increments of inches or centimeters (whichever you use). The most useful size is 2" x 18" (5 × 46 cm), although smaller ones can be handy, too. With these rulers, you can quickly measure parallel lines for hem allowances and pressing templates. Quilter's rulers are thicker and more rigid than artist's rulers, and they're great if you are cutting with a rotary cutter.

Pressing Gear

Frequent pressing keeps seams smooth and edges crisp. A good iron and a sturdy ironing board are as important for successful sewing as your sewing machine. It's always a good idea to steam-press your fabric before you cut it.

Iron: Work with a steam iron. It doesn't have to be expensive. You'll

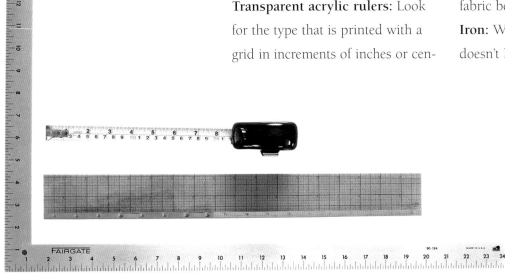

be pressing large areas and using lots of steam, so fill the iron with distilled water, which is less likely to stain than tap water should the iron spit.

Ironing board: A standard ironing board with a cotton cover is fine. Coated covers don't absorb the steam, so the fabric sometimes slides around on them. An iron-rest extension is a nice extra that frees up more of the board space for pressing.

Steamer: Definitely not essential, but a steamer can be handy for touch-ups after your window treatment is installed. Small hand-held steamers are inexpensive. Put a cotton sock over the nozzle to catch any drips.

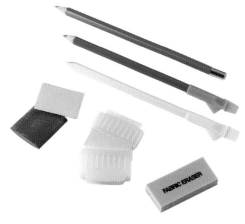

Marking Tools

There are several types of fabric markers. They all work well, but one type may be more effective on a certain fabric than another, so it's smart to have a variety on hand. Be sure to select a color that contrasts with your fabric. Think about how long you need the marks to last— just while you cut or throughout the whole sewing process? If you are marking on the right side of your fabric or marking a sheer fabric, always test to be sure the mark will disappear or can be removed as directed on the label.

Fabric-marking pens: These pens come in limited colors and are either water soluble (which means the ink stays on your fabric until you remove it by rubbing with a damp cloth) or air-soluble (which means the ink disappears on its own after a day or two).

Fabric-marking pencils: These pencils are made specifically for fabric and come in quite a few colors. Some are chalk, which makes soft lines that brush or rub off easily. Others have a harder lead, which makes sharp lines that must be washed out.

Chalk dispensers: These small containers are filled with powdered chalk, which is dispersed through a tiny opening and drawn with a wheel. They make sharp lines and they're fun to use!

Cutting Tools

You only need a few cutting tools, but the ones you have should be sharp enough to make clean cuts. You'll be cutting large pieces of fabric, so make sure your tools are comfortable to use.

Shears: These tools have offset handles that allow the blades to glide along the table as you cut. They are shaped specifically for right-handed or left-handed people. Have two sizes on hand: 9" or 10" (23 or 25.5 cm) for cutting out the project and 7" or 8" (18 or 20 cm) for clipping and trimming seam allowances. The larger the shears, the faster and cleaner the cutting.

Scissors: Scissors have blades centered between small loop handles. They are best for making small cuts and trimming thread. Have at least one small pair. Sewing scissors are about 6" (15 cm) long and have one blade with a rounded tip, which won't pierce the fabric, and one blade with a pointed tip. Embroidery scissors are small— about 4" (10 cm) long—and have fine, sharply pointed blades.

Seam ripper: Small and easy to handle, a seam ripper has a tiny crescent-shaped blade at the end of a plastic handle. The pointed end of the blade can pierce fabric or easily slide under a single stitch. The sharp curved part can slice a buttonhole open. It can also glide between fabric layers to cut a seam apart—but you need to be especially careful because it's easy to cut the fabric instead of the stitches.

Rotary cutter: This tool looks like a small pizza cutter with a very sharp blade. It's ideal for making straight cuts. You need to place the fabric on a cutting mat to protect the table surface. Mats that are large enough for window treatments are costly and cumbersome, so this tool may not be practical for all types of cutting.

Craft or utility knife and cutting mat: You'll need these tools (or a paper cutter) in order to cut the pressing templates (page 36) you'll need when making hems.

Sewing Gear

Keep your sewing machine in good working order and have needles in various sizes on hand. Find small boxes, tins, or pincushions to hold pins on your worktable and at the sewing machine and ironing board. Magnetic pincushions help keep the pins from spilling!

Sewing machine and presser feet: You don't need a fancy machine to make window treatments. A basic sewing machine with a few utility stitches is perfect. For some projects, you'll need a blind-hem foot, a zipper or cording foot, or a zigzag foot. Check your machine manual to see which type of sewing machine needle is best for the fabric you've chosen. Because some window treatments are large, it's a good idea to place your machine on a large table or in a machine table so that the fabric is supported as you work. Fabric that drags on the floor doesn't feed evenly and may tangle under your feet. If you have a serger, you can use it to finish fabric edges so they don't ravel, but the zigzag stitch on your regular machine works well, too.

Pins: Long sharp pins are easy to handle and insert through multiple

important is that the thread is appropriate for the type and weight of your fabric. Cotton or cotton-wrapped polyester thread is fine for most fabrics. Ask a salesperson for help if you're not sure what to buy.

Cord: You'll work with soft cotton or polyester cord as the filler when making fabric-covered cord. You can buy it in several thicknesses, depending on the size you need. You'll use sash cord, which is thin and sturdy, to rig draped valances like the tie-up, cloud, and balloon treatment styles featured in this book. Both types of cord are sold in packages and by the yard.

Rings: Valance styles that drape horizontally have small plastic rings sewn to the wrong side. You tie cord through these rings to create the draping. The rings come in packages, and you sew them on by hand.

Curtain weights: Small metal weights help curtains hang straight or keep them from blowing in the wind. You sew them to the bottom corners of long curtains (page 104), but rarely need them on valances. Purchase curtain weights that are covered with a lightweight, non-woven fabric that extends in a

fabric layers. Thin pins are fine for lightweight fabric. For heavier fabrics, use sturdier pins that won't bend. Glass-head pins are easy to see—so are T-pins, but they're too thick for some window treatment fabrics. Try them out to see.

Hand-sewing needles: Window treatments require very little hand-sewing, but it's a good idea to have an assortment of needles on hand in case you need them. The type labeled "sharps" is a good basic needle. Quilting needles or "betweens" are longer and have larger eyes than sharps. Embroidery needles have even larger eyes. All

types are sized by a numeral code—the higher the numeral, the thinner the needle. Purchase a package of mixed sizes or size 7 or 8, which are fine for most purposes.

Notions

You can't sew without thread! Purchase spools that match the color or pattern of your fabric. Some window treatments require special notions, which you can find at most large fabric stores, retail decorator fabric stores, and many home centers.

Thread: There's no special thread for window treatments. What's

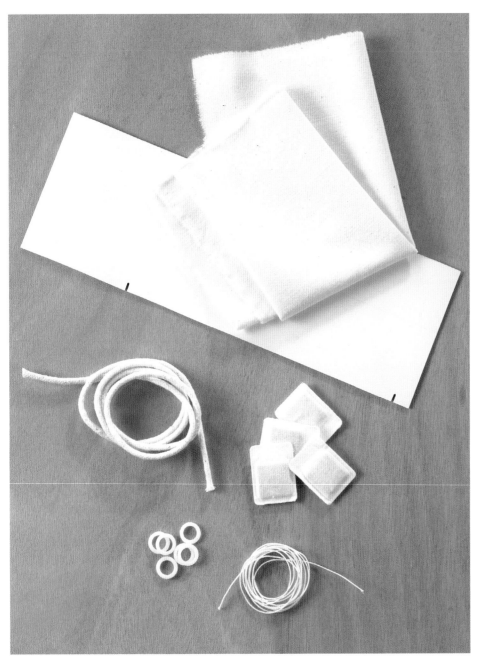

Clockwise from top: muslin, cardstock, curtain weights, sash cord, small plastic rings, and soft filler cord

sew-through flange. This type is much easier to attach to fabric than plain metal washers.

Muslin or brown paper: You'll need one or both of these materials to work out patterns for shaped hemlines.

Cardstock or poster board: These sturdy papers are perfect for making pressing templates (page 36).

Lining Fabric

Some of the window treatments in this book have a lining. A lining can be any type of lightweight (but not sheer) fabric—usually cotton or a cotton-polyester blend works well. To make your planning, cutting, and sewing easier, choose a lining that is the same width as the decorator fabric. Linings are visible from the outside of your windows, so if you have different treatments in different rooms, you might want them all to have the same lining to create a uniform look. If not, you can choose a lining color that compliments the decorator fabric. Prints are not a good choice because their pattern may show through the decorator fabric when the sun shines through them. White and off-white are less likely to affect the color or pattern of the decorator fabric.

Curtain Rods

There are many types of curtain rods, suitable for the different types of window treatment designs and installation. The rod pocket at the top of the window treatment conceals the standard curtain rod. Most rods have "returns"—a short section that extends back to the wall at each end. The returns are mounted on concealed brackets.

Rods come in various sizes and may be adjusted to span windows of different widths. Sometimes, the return depth is adjustable, too. Decorative rods have an ornament, which is called a finial, at each end. The brackets show and are part of the design. You can use this style of rod with rod pockets or fit the rods with rings that clip onto the curtain to make it easy to open and close. Decorative rods are not adjustable, but you can often cut them to size.

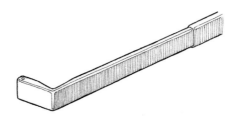

Standard curtain rods: *flat metal or acrylic rods.* The smallest is 1" (2.5 cm) wide (top to bottom measurement). You'll use the wider 2½" (6.4 cm) size for most of the projects in this book. Rods 4½" (11.4 cm) wide are also available. All types come in various adjustable lengths (along the horizontal dimension).

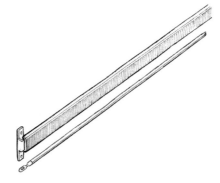

Sash rods: *slender flat or round rods with very shallow brackets that protrude only ¼" (6 mm).* Sash rods can be positioned on doors or right on the window sash. To keep sash curtains taut, place rods at the top and bottom of the window and sew a rod pocket at the bottom and top of the curtain.

Spring tension rods: *adjustable slender rods that fit inside the window recess.* There are several styles. Most have a rubber cap at each end to protect the woodwork of the window frame. Just be sure to install them so they don't interfere with the window operation.

Decorative rods: *wood or metal rods, in many diverse styles and finishes.* Café rods are slender rods, usually white enamel or brass, with small, unobtrusive brackets. The rods may come with rings (often with clips to hold the curtains), which are also sold separately.

measuring and planning

Every window treatment begins
with accurate measurements and
detailed planning. The steps aren't
hard—they just require a little
thought. If you measure and plan
correctly, the sewing will be easy,
and your treatment will look just
the way you dreamed it would.

Measuring the Window

You should measure each window that you want to cover, even if all the windows look as if they're the same. Work with a retractable steel measuring tape and ask someone to help you. Follow the diagram below and record each dimension as you measure.

If you are making treatments for several windows in the same room, measure the distance from window to window and the distance to the adjacent wall or doorway. These measurements will help you plan how wide to make the treatment. (Take measurements H and I after you decide whether you are making inside- or outside-mounted window treatments.)

Outside Mount

For outside-mounted curtains, decide how far the treatment will extend beyond the window molding (H on the diagram). The measurement from H to H is the **horizontal wall space**. Outside-mounted valances should extend only far enough beyond the molding so you can install the brackets on the wall (as for Valance with Tucked Hem, shown on page 42). Decide how far above the window the rod will be installed. The standard position is level with the top of the molding. If you want the rod to be higher, record that dimension as measurement I.

If you have a U-shaped rod, measure the depth of the side (which is called the **return**). Add twice this amount to the horizontal wall space for both returns.

Inside Mount

For an inside-mounted curtain or valance, the sash width is the horizontal wall space. The sash length is the maximum length of the finished treatment. Make sure the jamb is deep enough to hold the curtain rod and still allow the sash to operate (C on the diagram).

Measuring from Hardware

If the mounting hardware is already installed, refer to the diagram below at right. Measure the width of the rod from bracket to bracket, including any returns. If you have a decorative rod with finials, the horizontal wall space for your treat-

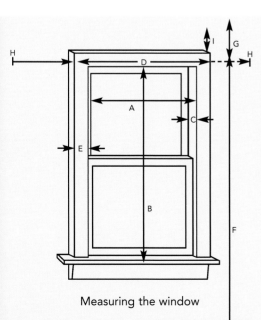

A: Inside (sash) width
B: Inside (sash) length
C: Inside reveal (depth of jamb)
D: Outside width
E: Molding width
F: Outside length to floor
G: Top of molding to ceiling
H: Side extension: outside of
    molding to side of treatment
I: Top extension: top of molding
    to top of treatment

Measuring the window

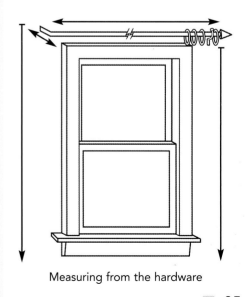

Measuring from the hardware

ment can be no wider than the bracket-to-bracket distance. If you are hanging your treatment from rings, however, you can usually position one ring on the outside of each bracket, so the wall space extends to the inside of the finials. Measure the finished length from the top of the rod. If you are using rings, measure from the top of the clip at the bottom of the ring.

Project Planning Guide

You can't make a window treatment without doing some arithmetic—but the calculations aren't difficult. First, you need to decide how the treatment will cover your window so you can figure out how big it should be. The easiest way to do this is to make some sketches. The drawings don't have to be perfect—they are just tools to help you plan.

You can work with one of these sample sketches at right as a guide to plan every project in this book. Sketch A shows a valance. Sketch B shows a pair of floor-length curtains. (Both curtains will be identical, so you only need to plan the size of one.)

When sketching, you'll work with the finished dimensions of the window treatment—the width and length of the completed treatment when it is lying flat. Finished dimensions don't include the seam allowances, the rod pocket facing, or the hem allowances. You will add those allowances later, during the planning process (step 7).

Standard or Metric Measurements?

The dimensions in this book have been calculated for easy measuring and sewing in both the standard (also known as English) and metric systems. The equivalents are not consistent because they have been rounded up or down to make the best sense for each part of the process. Refer to only one system as you work.

Step 1: Draw a Sketch

Make a sketch of your window. Now draw the style of treatment you've chosen on the sketch. If the treatment will be outside mounted, be sure the drawing spans the window trim. If it will be inside mounted, make the window trim visible.

If the fabric will be gathered on the rod, draw a series of vertical

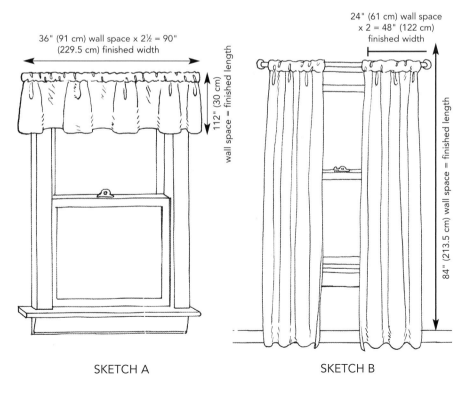

SKETCH A

SKETCH B

lines to indicate the gathers. Refer to your window measurements, and make notes on the sketch to indicate how much of the horizontal and vertical wall space the treatment will cover.

Fullness is the amount of fabric that is gathered onto the rod when you hang the treatment. If you know how much fullness you want, indicate that on the drawing, too. (If you don't know, see Calculating Fullness at right. Add the calculation to your sketch when you complete step 3.)

Now you can figure the dimensions of your treatment. We'll use the valance (sketch A) as a sample to explain the process. According to the sketch for the sample valance, the horizontal wall space is 36" (91 cm). For fullness, you will need 2½ times that measurement. So, the finished window treatment will be 90" (229.5 cm).

The vertical wall space on the sample sketch is 12" (30 cm). The vertical space is usually the finished length of the window treatment. If you want your valance to drape or your curtains to "puddle" on the floor, you need to add more length (the instructions for the long curtain

calculating fullness

Fullness is the amount of fabric that is gathered across a curtain or valance when it hangs on the window. Most often, a window treatment is 2 or 2½ times as wide as the window or horizontal wall space. This relationship is expressed as a ratio: the amount of fabric to the width of the area to be covered.

Lightweight fabrics can be more tightly gathered onto a rod than heavier fabrics. Usually, treatments made of lightweight fabric have a fullness of 3 to 1. Medium-weight fabric requires a fullness of 2½ or 2 to 1. Heavyweight fabric requires a fullness of 1½ or 2 to 1.

Fullness is also part of the design, however, so you can really choose whatever amount of fullness you like. The amount of fullness determines whether the treatment hangs flat, is slightly fluted, or is dense with folds.

Why do you need to decide the fullness? If the finished width of your window treatment is wider than your fabric, you'll need to sew together two pieces of fabric. So, you'll have to know the finished width ahead of time so you can buy enough yardage for two cut lengths.

How exact does the ratio need to be? For simple window treatments (like the projects in this book), you can approximate the fullness ratio. You just want to have a general idea of the fullness so you know how many pieces of fabric you need to sew together to get the look you want. You don't need to buy extra fabric or cut any off to achieve a perfect ratio. Your window treatment will look just fine as long as the fullness is close to the ratio you've chosen.

projects in the book indicate how much to add).

Step 2: Determine the Cut Length

Add the top and bottom allowances to the finished length you've noted on the sketch. The bottom allowance is for the hem. Depending on the style of treatment you've chosen, the top allowance might be for a hem, a rod-pocket facing, or

a seam. The instructions for each project indicate the specific allowances you need.

For the sample valance, the finished length is 12" (30 cm), the top allowance is 6" (15 cm), and the bottom allowance is 5" (13 cm). Add these together to determine the cut length—23" (58 cm).

Adjust the cut length for patterned fabric: When working with patterned fabric, you need extra yardage so that you can match the pattern when you join panels to get a wider width. Or, if you're making the same treatment for several windows, you'll need extra fabric so that you can place the motifs in the same position on each one. You want the motifs to align horizontally around the room. Here's how to adjust the cut length of patterned fabric.

First, find the size of the pattern repeat. To do this, measure lengthwise from a specific point on one motif (the center of a flower, for instance) to the same point on the next identical motif.

Next, divide the cut length by the length of the repeat. Round up to the next whole number. This number is the number of repeats to allow for each length of fabric needed.

Last, multiply the number of repeats needed per length by the length of the repeat. Use this number as the cut length when you figure the yardage in step 5.

For example, if the cut length is 90" (230 cm) and the repeat is 20" (51 cm), these are your calculations:

90" ÷ 20" = 4.5
(230 ÷ 51 cm = 4.5)
Round up to 5 repeats needed per length.
5 repeats × 20" = 100"
(5 repeats × 51 cm = 255 cm)

The total is the adjusted cut length. If the repeat length is greater than your cut length—on a valance, for example—the adjusted cut length is the repeat length.

Step 3: Determine the Finished Width

To find the finished width of your treatment, multiply the horizontal wall space that you've noted on your sketch by the amount of fullness you've chosen for your fabric or your design (2, 2½, or 3). Add the calculation to your sketch, as shown in the examples on page 26.

Step 4: Determine the Number of Fabric Lengths You Need

For this step, you need to know the width of your fabric so you can do the calculation. Divide the finished width of the treatment (step 3) by the fabric width. Round up to the next whole number. This number tells you the number of lengths you have to sew together to achieve the total width you need for the window treatment.

For example, for our sample valance, the finished width is 90" (229.5 cm) and the fabric width is 54" (137 cm).

planning a rod pocket

The rod pocket should be slightly larger than the rod so that the fabric slides over the rod easily. For a flat rod, make the pocket about ½" (1.5 cm) deeper than the vertical dimension of the rod. This extra depth is enough to accommodate the rod thickness, which is minimal. For a round rod, measure the circumference of the rod, divide in half, and add ½" (1.5 cm) to find the pocket depth.

When a curtain is hung on a round rod, it is a little shorter than when it is flat, because the rod diameter "takes up" some of the length. To adjust for this shortness, find the difference between half the rod circumference and the rod diameter. Add it to the cut length measurement when you plan your project. The difference won't be a lot, but it's worth including in the length.

math at a glance

A = Cut length of treatment
B = Amount of fullness desired (1½, 2, 2½, or 3 times the horizontal wall space)

B × Horizontal wall space = Finished width of treatment
Finished width ÷ Fabric width = Number of fabric lengths needed
A × Number of lengths needed = Total length in inches (centimeters)
Total length in inches ÷ 36 = Yards of fabric required
(Total length in centimeters ÷ 100 = Meters of fabric required)

90" ÷ 54" = 1.66
(229.5 ÷ 137 cm = 1.66)
1.66 rounded to the next whole number = 2

So we need two lengths of fabric to get the finished width we need for the valance.

Confused? Don't worry. Just complete this step and continue. The process will make more sense when you've worked through the next steps.

Step 5: Calculate the Yardage

Now you'll calculate how many yards of fabric you need to buy. This is easy. Multiply the cut length, or, for patterned fabric, multiply the adjusted cut length (step 2) by the number of lengths you need (step 4) to find the total length in inches. Divide that number by 36", which

is equal to 1 yd., to find the yardage. (Divide by 100 cm to find the number of meters.)

For the sample valance, the cut length is 23" (68 cm). In step 4, we determined that we need two lengths.

23" × 2 lengths = 46"
(58 cm × 2 = 116 cm)
46" ÷ 36" = 1.27 yd.
(116 ÷ 100 cm = 1.16 m)

Fabric is sold in ⅛- or ⅓-yd. increments (or 10-cm increments), so round the numbers up for a total of 1⅓ yd. (1.4 m).

If your project has small pieces (like tabs or tiebacks) or if your fabric is patterned, complete step 6 before you buy your fabric. Add the cut dimensions of each piece to the layout sketch. Then add up the noted dimensions to double-check that the pieces fit on the fabric as

here's a hint!

If your project requires more than one fabric, make a layout sketch for each one—just as shown in the project instructions.

you've sketched them and that the total length is the same as your yardage calculation in step 5.

Step 6: Check the Cutting Layout

Now you'll figure out how the pieces of your project will be arranged on the fabric for cutting.

Every project in this book has a sketch that shows the layout for the project's finished size and fabric width. But if you are making a different size, or your fabric is a different width, you'll want to make your own sketch, using the project sketch as a guide.

here's a hint!

The top, side, and bottom allowances are added to the finished dimensions of the window treatment. An allowance is the amount of fabric that is folded to the wrong side of your project.

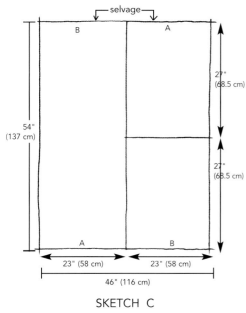

SKETCH C

Sketch C shows the cutting layout for our sample valance. Based on the calculations in step 4, we need two lengths of fabric for the valance, sewn together to make one piece of wide fabric. Simple. So why make a sketch? If you simply cut the fabric into two lengths and sew them together, you will have a seam running up the middle of the valance. Not so nice.

Instead, cut one of the lengths in half vertically and sew one half to each side of the full-width piece. Always sew together the selvage edges—in other words, don't sew the cut edge of the half-width piece to the selvage of the full-width piece. You'll sew together the edges marked A in the example sketch and also the edges marked B. The cut edges of the fabric become the side edges of the valance.

Step 7: Check the Assembly and Allowances

You'll be able to work faster if you understand how the pieces go together and if you know the size of each seam allowance and hem

here's a hint!

When you purchase your fabric, have it rolled on a cylindrical bolt. It will be easier to manipulate as you're cutting.

allowance. Each project in this book lists the seam allowances needed. You may want to sketch the assembly in order to visualize the allowances. Sketch D is an example of how to do this for our sample valance. It shows the window treatment pieces spread out flat. If you decide to make your own sketch, don't worry if it isn't in perfect proportion—it's just for reference.

The full-width piece of fabric is in the middle, and the half-widths are on each side.

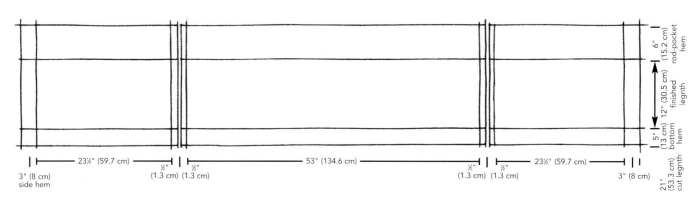

SKETCH D

If you are making more than one of a treatment and want the fabric motifs to fall in the same place on each, cut out the first treatment. Then use the pieces as a pattern for the others, aligning the motifs carefully.

- The seam allowances where these pieces are joined are indicated as ½" (2 cm). That means there's a ½" (2 cm) seam allowance on each piece of fabric.
- The side hem allowance is 3" (8 cm). That means there is one hem on each vertical edge.
- The rod-pocket hem at the top is 6" (16 cm).
- The bottom hem allowance is 5" (13 cm).

Marking and Cutting

Accurate cutting sets the stage for successful sewing. Because most pieces for window treatments are just rectangles, you rarely use a pattern for cutting. Instead, you just measure and mark the outline of each piece directly on the fabric. Work on a large table so you can spread out the fabric in one layer—you'll need to be able to measure and mark all sections of each piece.

Keep everything square

Fabric is woven from two sets of threads that are perpendicular to each other. The threads form a lengthwise straight grain and a crosswise straight grain. The lengthwise threads are parallel to the selvage (the finished edge) of the fabric. The 45-degree angle between the lengthwise and crosswise grains is the bias. The straight grains are stable, which means they don't stretch. The bias naturally stretches when pulled by the sewer or by gravity. The drawing below shows the grainlines.

In order for a window treatment to hang correctly, every piece you mark and cut must be oriented correctly on the fabric. In most cases, the vertical edges fall on the lengthwise straight grain of the fabric, and the horizontal edges fall on the crosswise grain. Most fabric patterns are woven or printed with this orientation in mind.

Sometimes it makes sense to cut the vertical edges of a piece on the crosswise grain—for example, to orient a lengthwise stripe pattern horizontally on the window instead of vertically. The term for this is railroading. For a short window treatment, railroading allows you to cut the treatment in one piece, instead of cutting and joining several pieces to get the width you need.

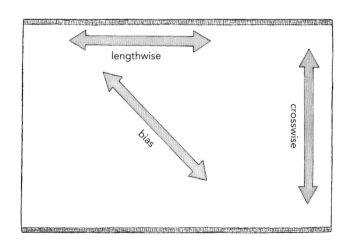

If the cut length of the piece (page 28) is greater than the width of the fabric, however, you won't be able to railroad it.

Fabric for decorative accents, such as covered cord or bows, may be cut on the bias. For covered cord, the stretch of the bias makes the fabric fit smoothly around the cord. For bows, the bias may enhance the drape of the loops and tails. Accents made of bias-cut stripes or plaids visually separate from the straight-grain background pieces, yet coordinate perfectly.

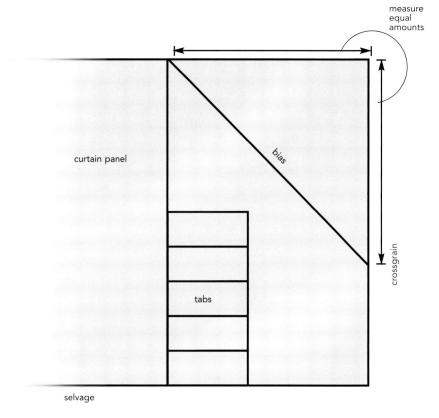

Measuring to find the bias

Refer to the planning diagrams

Spread the fabric. Refer to your planning sketches (pages 26 and 30) and the sample cutting layout for each project to determine the dimensions and orientation of each piece. Measure and mark the cutting lines. To mark horizontal cutting lines, place one leg of an L-square on the selvage and draw along the other leg. Extend the L-square with a long straightedge as a guide. To mark vertical cutting lines, measure from the selvage and mark at two or more places. Connect the marks with a long straightedge as a guide.

Cutting bias pieces

Lay your fabric flat so you can find the bias (45 degrees from the selvage). To do this, measure and mark an equal distance on the selvage and the crossgrain. How far to measure depends on the area of fabric available—measure the longest distance possible. Draw a bias line between the marks, as shown in the drawing above.

Working with a transparent gridded ruler as a guide, mark one or more lines parallel to the bias line. Space these lines at the interval

needed for the bias strip width in your project. Measure the total length of the marked strips to be sure you have enough. Allow some extra for sewing the strips together to make one long piece. Cut on all the marked lines.

preparing shaped hemlines

If you are making a valance with a shaped lower edge, you'll need to make a pattern for it. The easiest way to do this is to first draw a half-pattern of the shape. Whether your valance is flat or has fullness, first make a half-pattern that has no fullness. Then, to add fullness, cut this pattern into several pieces and spread them apart to the width you need (see Calculating Fullness on page 27).

In this book, the projects with shaped hemlines include diagrams for drafting this pattern. To explain the process, the example below shows how to shape half a scalloped valance that is the same length in the center as at the sides.

1. Draw your pattern on a large piece of paper or muslin. First draw the top line, making it equal to half the horizontal wall width to be covered by your valance (page 26). If the valance has fullness, exclude the returns. If it is flat, include them.

Refer to the diagram to draw the side, center fold, and bottom edges. Work with a flexible ruler to create the hem line shape you like, or with a piece of string held in place with tape. Draw perpendicular lines with an L-square as a guide. Mark the edges as "side" and "center."

2. Cut out the pattern. Hold it up to your window to be sure you like the shape of the bottom edge. Adjust it by redrawing (tape on more paper if you need to). For a flat valance, proceed to step 5.

3. On a larger piece of paper or muslin, draw a line equal to half the finished width of your valance (page 28). If your valance has returns, multiply the depth of the return by the fullness you're using. Mark this distance at one end of the line. For example, if the return is 4" (10 cm) and the fullness is 2, you should mark 8" (20 cm) from the end of the line.

4. Draw parallel vertical lines at 2" (5 cm) intervals on your cutout pattern. Number the sections and cut the pattern apart on the lines. Arrange the cutout pieces in sequence on the larger paper, aligning their top edges with the drawn line and spacing them equally across, as shown in the drawing below at right. Do not place any pieces on the return.

Draw a new bottom line that passes gracefully across the longest part of each cutout section and extends straight across the return (if there is one). Adjust the shape of the bottom line if you wish.

5. Add the rod-pocket, side, and bottom allowances for your project and cut out the pattern.

When making the valance, cut the fabric pieces as rectangles with the greatest length needed. Don't cut the shaped lower edge. First, sew the pieces together to get the needed width. Then fold the joined piece in half at the vertical center. Now use the pattern to cut the lower edge.

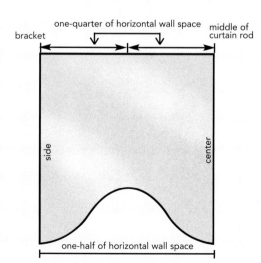

Half-pattern without fullness

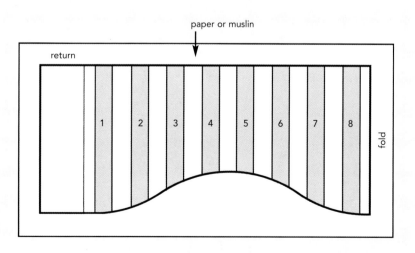

Half-pattern with fullness

sewing essentials

After you have cut the fabric for your project, the next essential step is assembly—which includes pinning, pressing, and sewing. You may be surprised to find you spend more time pinning and pressing than you do actually feeding the fabric through the machine. After all, the sewing machine has a motor and will make quick work of every seam! Pinning and pressing accurately will guarantee great sewn results.

Pinning

When you're making a window treatment, you'll be sewing long seams, and the big pieces of fabric may be awkward to handle. Pinning before sewing is a smart move—the pins keep the fabric layers aligned as you carry the project from your work surface to the ironing board or sewing machine, and they keep the fabric in place while you're sewing, too.

To pin, always lay the pieces on your work surface, spreading them as flat as you can (pinning in your lap isn't very accurate). Orient the pieces so the edges to be pinned together are closest to you. Spread one layer of fabric first, then lay the next on top of it.

Place pins perpendicular to the seam, across the seamline, with the pinheads toward the cut edge of the fabric, as shown in the top photo, or toward the outside fold of a hem, as shown in the bottom photo. The heads should be to the right of the needle as you sew—this makes them easy to pull out as they approach the presser foot. If you're not sure which way to place the pin heads, just remember that when you sew, the largest part of the

project will be to the left side of the needle and the seam allowance or hem to the right.

You might be tempted to sew over pins as you're stitching, but this is not a good idea. The needle might hit the pin and break, or you might stitch a small tuck in one of the fabric layers. Keep a small box or tin on the machine table to put the pins in as you pull them out.

Pressing

As you sew, press your work frequently to smooth the fabric layers and make a crisp edge on folds. Be sure to use the heat and steam setting recommended for your fabric. Window treatments are large, and professionals work with a big pressing table instead of an ironing board so they can spread out the fabric and press long seams. To give yourself the largest possible pressing area, rotate your ironing board 180 degrees and press on the wide end—but be careful when resting your iron on the narrow end.

Pins and pressing

It's usually best not to press over pins. There's a chance that you'll press a permanent impression of the pin into your fabric. If you need to press while the project is pinned, pin and press a scrap to test for damage. If there is a mark, you can gently slide the tip of the iron around the pins.

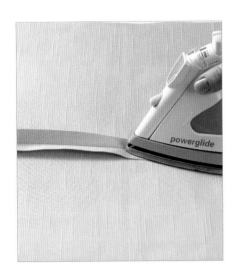

board or even a cereal box. Make them 10" to 12" (25 to 30 cm) long and as deep as you need to for your project. You may even need several sizes for one project. To make the template edges smooth, cut with a utility knife or craft knife on a self-healing cutting mat, working with a straightedge as a guide.

Pressing seam allowances open

If, according to the project instructions, you need to press the seam allowances open after sewing a seam, place the project wrong side up on the ironing board. Separate the allowances with your fingers and then slide the iron tip along the seam to fold the allowances flush with the fabric, as shown in the photo above.

Pressing seam allowances to one side

If your project instructions say to press the seam allowances in a single direction (for example, toward the lining), place the project wrong side up on the ironing board and press the allowances open. Then fold the allowances together in the direction indicated and slide the tip of the iron along the seam to press them flush with the fabric, as shown in the photo above.

Pressing templates

Cardboard pressing templates make it easy to fold and press a hem or facing. You don't need to measure and mark your fabric or use a hem gauge. The templates create a sharp crease, too. You can make templates from any noncorrugated, lightweight cardboard, such as poster

Pressing a double hem

To prepare a double hem, make a lightweight cardboard template about 12" (30 cm) long by the depth indicated in your project (which is twice the desired depth of the finished hem). For example, for a 3" (8 cm) hem, make a 6" × 12" (16 × 30 cm) template.

Lay your fabric wrong side up on your ironing board, with the edge to be hemmed facing you. Fold up and press the fabric over the template, aligning the fabric edge with the top of the template and making the crease along the bottom of the template, as shown in the top left photo on the facing page.

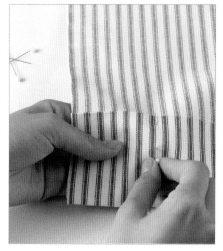

Open out the fabric and then fold it so the cut edge aligns with the pressed crease. Press the new fold, being careful not to press out the first crease, as shown in the photo below.

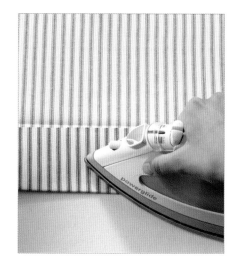

Remove the template. Fold the fabric again along the first crease. Pin through all three layers, placing the pins perpendicular to the second crease as shown in the photo above.

Pressing a single hem

To prepare a single hem, make two 12" (30 cm)-long lightweight cardboard templates, one in each depth indicated in the instructions for your project. (One should be the desired depth of the finished hem and the other should be 1" (2 cm) deeper than the desired depth of the finished hem.) For example, for a 3" (8 cm) hem, make one template 3" × 12" (8 × 30 cm) and one 4" × 12" (10 × 30 cm).

Lay your fabric wrong side up on your ironing board, with the edge to be hemmed toward you. Fold up

and press the fabric over the deeper template, aligning the fabric edge with the top of the template and making the crease along the bottom of the template, as shown in the photo above.

Open the fabric and place the narrower template on the hem allowance, aligning one edge of the template with the crease you just made. Fold the extending hem allowance up and over the tem-

plate. Press the new fold along the edge of the template.

Remove the template. Fold the fabric again along the first crease. Pin through all three layers, placing the pins perpendicular to the second crease.

Machine-sewing

To sew window treatments, all you need is a basic machine that sews a straight stitch. Zigzag stitches provide a way to finish the cut edge of fabric. A serger, if you have one, is a good alternative for zigzag stitching. If your machine has a blindstitch, you'll be able to sew an invisible hem. If you are trying out new stitches, make some practice seams with fabric scraps before sewing your project.

Conventional seam

When you need to join two pieces of fabric, place the pieces right sides together, aligning the edges to be joined. (You would do the same to join opposite edges of the same piece, for example, to make a tab or tie). Pin the layers (page 35) and then sew them together with the seam allowance indicated—almost always ½" (2 cm) for the projects in this book. This means when you sew, you should keep the edge of the fabric aligned with the appropriate seam allowance guide on the machine throat plate. Always backstitch at the beginning and end of a seam to secure the stitches.

Edge finish

To keep fabric from raveling, sew along the cut edge with a zigzag stitch or another of the utility stitches on your machine. Set the stitch to a medium width and length. Sew a test on a piece of scrap fabric. The fabric should stay flat. If it puckers, adjust the settings. If you have a serger, you can overlock the edge instead of zigzagging.

You don't need to finish edges that will be hemmed. You also don't need to finish edges that will be covered by a lining, unless the fabric is very loosely woven.

Topstitched hem

Place the pressed and pinned hem wrong side up in the bed of your machine. Position it so the needle is on the hem, very close to the edge to be stitched, with the hem extending to the right of the presser foot. Set the machine to a medium-long straight stitch. Sew along the edge of the hem. Remember—the other side of the project is the one that will be visible, so make sure the bobbin thread is the right color and the thread tension is correct. Sew a test on a scrap and adjust the stitch to a length you like.

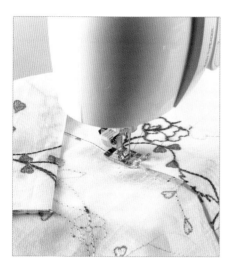

clipping and trimming

Corners and curved edges should be neat and crisp when they're turned right side out, so trim the excess seam allowance in these areas to eliminate bulk.

To trim a corner, cut the seam allowance diagonally, as shown in the photo at right. For a corner or point that is less than 90 degrees, cut the allowance at a sharper diagonal so it will fit smoothly when the corner is turned right side out. You can cut close to the point. When you turn the corner, gently push out the point with a slender, blunt object.

To trim an outside curve, cut a series of small notches from the seam allowance. You want to make the allowance fit smoothly inside the curve after it is turned right side out, so the number and spacing of the notches depend on the size of the curve. Test the effect by folding the allowance over, onto the project, along the seamline. Be very neat when you do this—the seam allowance may show through along the turned edge.

To trim an inside curve, simply make the seam allowance narrower along the curved area. In most cases, the curved area will have enough bias for the narrow allowance to stretch around the curve when the piece is turned right side out. Test the effect by folding the allowance over, onto the project, along the seamline. If the curve is too tight, the allowance may not be able to stretch enough. If so, clip the allowance at intervals, cutting straight across the allowance and stopping just before the stitching.

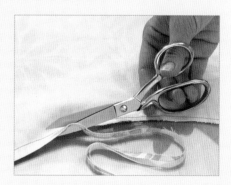

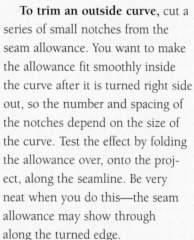

simple
designs

When you're talking about window treatments, simple never means dull. Each of the simple projects in this chapter has a special detail that gives it a classy finish. They are so appealing, you may be surprised to see that each is really just a simple rectangle of fabric that is hemmed on all four edges. Window décor doesn't get any easier than this. As long as you can sew a straight seam, you can make all of these projects with great success. If you're a new sewer, these projects are the perfect place to try out your skills and build confidence. If you're experienced, you'll love how these designs make it easy to dress your windows in style.

valance with tucked hem

The pretty tuck at the top of the hem gives this valance a delicate detail—and it couldn't be easier to make. In fact, it's easier than making a neat conventional hem. Choose a fabric that holds a crease when pressed, and the valance will snap right into shape.

The Sample

- Shown in medium-weight polka-dot-printed satin-stripe cotton
- Fullness: 1½ times the horizontal wall space (including returns)
- Finished dimensions: 75" wide × 15" long (191 × 38 cm)

Supplies

- curtain rod (shown 2½" [6.5 cm] deep with 4½" [11.5 cm] returns)
- thread
- pins
- scissors
- L-square and long straightedge
- pressing templates: 6" (16 cm), 5" (13 cm), and 3" (8 cm) deep (page 36)

Allowances

- Rod-pocket hem allowance: 6" (16 cm)
- Bottom hem allowance, including 1" (2 cm) for the tuck: 3½" (9 cm)
- Joining seam allowance (if needed to join widths, add to each piece): ½" (2 cm)
- Side hem allowance (add to each vertical edge): 3" (8 cm)

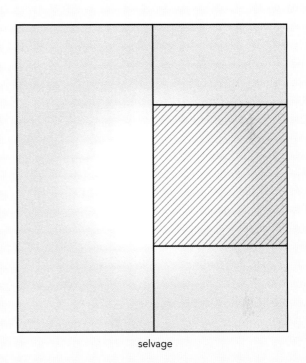

selvage

Measure, Plan, Buy Fabric

Determine the mounting style (page 14) and measure the window (page 25). Calculate your valance dimensions and determine the yardage (page 29). Figure the cut length, adding the rod-pocket and bottom hem allowances.

If you use a different-size curtain rod than the one indicated, plan the rod-pocket allowance to fit (page 28). Refer to the cutting layout above to help you plan.

valance with tucked hem

1 Cut out the fabric pieces for the valance, as described on page 43. If you need to join two or more pieces of fabric to get the right width, sew them together with ½" (2 cm) seam allowances. Press the seam allowances open.

2 To prepare the bottom hem and tuck, fold up and press the bottom edge as if you were making a double hem (page 36). Work with the 5" (13 cm)-deep template.

3 Instead of pinning the first crease to the valance for a double hem, pin the fabric through all layers close to the second crease, as shown in the photo. Leave the first crease loose. The second crease will become the tuck, and the first crease will fold down to become the hem. To make it easier to remove the pins when sewing, place them perpendicular to the second crease, with the heads toward the crease.

4 Place the valance on the bed of your sewing machine, wrong side up. Align the pinned folded edge with the ½" (1 cm) seam guide on the throat plate (this distance determines the depth of the tuck).

5 Sew through all layers with a medium-length straight stitch. Keep the fold aligned with the guide and pull out the pins as you go. You've just sewn the hem and the tuck at the same time!.

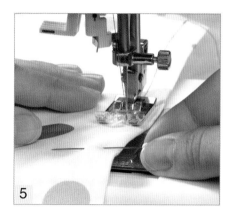

6 Lay the valance right side up on your ironing board, with the hem extending below the tuck. Fold the tuck down, onto the hem, and press.

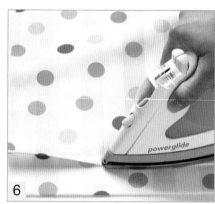

7 Turn the valance wrong side up on the ironing board. Working with the 3" (8 cm) template, press a double hem on one side edge (page 36)—the finished hem will be 1½" (4 cm) deep. Pin the double hem perpendicular to the second crease.

8 Rotate the valance and then fold, press, and pin a double hem on the other side edge in the same way.

9 Sew one of the side hems (see Topstitched Hem, page 39). Stitch over the hem tuck carefully so it stays flat (you won't be able to see the part that's under the valance). Sew the other side hem in the same way.

10 Press and sew a double hem for the rod pocket, as shown in the sidebar at right. Use the 6" (16 cm) pressing template.

11 Slide the curtain rod into the rod pocket, gathering the valance onto the rod. If the rod has returns, make sure the inside of the rod is oriented toward the wrong side of the valance. Place the rod in its brackets—or inside the window if you've chosen a tension rod.

Pretty cute! Make more valances in other fun fabrics.

sewing a hem or rod pocket

A rod pocket is just a hem that is open at both ends so you can slip the rod inside. Always sew the side hems on the curtain or valance before you press and sew the rod pocket. The ends of the pocket will be smooth and secure—and it will be easier to insert the rod! For most fabrics, make a double hem for the rod pocket, as shown for this project. If your project fabric is heavy, you might want to make a single hem to avoid bulk. If so, press the hem as described on page 37.

1. Lay the fabric wrong side up on the ironing board, with the edge to be hemmed facing toward you. The project instructions will tell you which template you need for the rod pocket. Fold up the hem over the template, aligning the fabric edge with the top edge of the template. Press the fold with the iron, creasing the fabric as shown in the photo above.

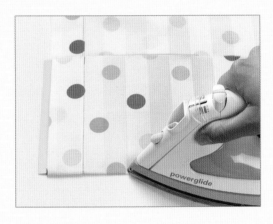

2. Unfold the fabric and remove the template. Fold again so the cut edge aligns with the pressed crease, as shown in the photo above. Press the new fold, being careful not to press out the first crease.

3. Fold the fabric again along the first crease. Pin through all three layers, placing the pins perpendicular to the second crease, as shown in the photo above.

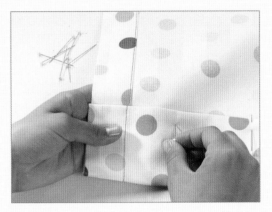

4. Place the project on the bed of your sewing machine, wrong side up, with the rod pocket to the right of the presser foot and the pinned fold under the foot. Sew through all layers with a medium straight stitch, stitching close to the pinned fold, as shown in the photo above. Pull out the pins as you go. Backstitch by making a few reverse stitches at the beginning and end of the seam to strengthen it.

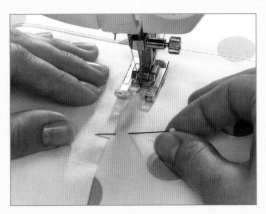

café curtains and valance

This sweet duet is similar to the Valance with Tucked Hem on page 42, but all the pieces have a heading—which looks like a small ruffle—at the top of the rod pocket. All three pieces are made in the same way, so complete each step on each piece before moving on to the next step.

The Sample
- Shown in lightweight plaid silk taffeta
- Fullness: 2½ times the horizontal wall space
- Finished valance dimensions: 90" wide by 13" long (229 × 33 cm)
- Finished curtain dimensions (each panel): 44" wide by 31" long (112 × 79 cm)

Supplies
- curtain rods (tension style is shown)
- thread
- pins
- scissors
- L-square and long straightedge
- pressing templates: 7" (18 cm), 5" (13 cm), and 3" (8 cm) deep (page 36)
- masking tape

Allowances
- Rod-pocket/heading hem allowance: 5" (13 cm)
- Bottom hem allowance (includes 1" [2 cm] for the tuck): 5" (13 cm)
- Joining seam allowance (if needed, add to each piece): ½" (2 cm)
- Side hem allowance (add to each vertical edge): 3" (8 cm)

Measure, Plan, Buy Fabric
Determine mounting style for your valance (page 14) and measure the window (page 25). Calculate the valance and curtain dimensions and determine the yardage (page 29). Figure the cut length, adding the rod-pocket and bottom hem allowances. If you use a different-size curtain rod than the one indicated, plan the rod-pocket allowance to fit (page 28). Refer to the cutting layout below to help you plan.

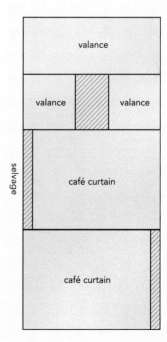

café curtains and valance

1 Cut out the fabric pieces for the valance and café curtains, as described on page 47. If you need to join two or more pieces of fabric to get the right width, sew them together. Press the seam allowances open.

here's a hint!

If you are using a checked fabric like the one shown here, plan so that the bottom of the valance and curtains fall along the edge of a check. That means the bottom of the check should be 5" (13 cm) above the cut bottom edge of the piece.

2 Press and sew a tucked hem at the bottom of each piece, working with the 5" (13 cm) pressing template and following steps 2 through 5 of the Valance with Tucked Hem on page 44.

3 Lay the valance right side up on your ironing board, with the hem extending below the tuck. Fold the tuck down, onto the hem, and press.

4 Press and sew a double hem on each vertical edge of each piece, using the 3" (8 cm) pressing template and following steps 7 through 9 of Valance with Tucked Hem on page 44.

5 Sew the rod pocket and heading, as explained on the facing page. Use the 7" (18 cm) pressing template. The heading depth is 2" (5 cm).

6 Slide each curtain rod into its rod pocket, gathering the valance onto one rod and the two curtains onto the second rod. If the rod has returns, make sure the inside of the rod is oriented toward the wrong side of the project. Place the rod in its brackets or inside the window if it is a tension rod.

don't want the tuck?

To make your valance without the tuck, simply sew a topstitched hem at the bottom and the sides. Add 3" (7.5 cm) to the finished length for the bottom hem. Prepare a double hem on the bottom edge (pages 36–37), using the 3" (7.5 cm) pressing template. Topstitch the hem.

Try different, coordinated, fabrics for valance and curtains.

sewing a rod pocket with a heading

A heading is a portion of the rod pocket that extends above the curtain rod. The pocket is deeper than it would be if there were no heading. Simply sew across it twice, once to secure the hem edge and again at a specified distance below the top of the project. The stitching will divide the pocket into two channels—one for the rod and another that forms a ruffle above the rod when the window treatment is installed. The instructions for each project will tell you the heading depth and the template size for pressing the rod pocket.

1. To begin, press and sew a rod pocket (same as a double hem) at the top of your project. Work with the pressing template indicated in the project instructions. (Refer to the sidebar on page 45 if you're not sure how to do this.)

2. Check your project instructions to see how deep to make the heading. If the depth is greater than the largest seam allowance guide marked on your sewing machine throat plate, make a guide (it's easy) so you'll be able to sew parallel to the edge. Here's what you do:

Subtract ½" (1 cm) from the specified heading depth and note the total. On the bed of your machine, add a distance equal to the total amount to the right of the ½" (1 cm) seam guide. Place a piece of masking tape on the bed of the machine at that point. Check with a transparent gridded ruler or a hem gauge to make sure the tape is parallel to the other seam guides, as shown below.

3. Place the sewn rod pocket in the machine so that its top fold is aligned with the appropriate seam allowance guide or your tape guide. Sew, keeping the fold aligned with the guide. Back-stitch by making a few reverse stitches at the beginning and end of the seam to strengthen it, as shown below.

here's a hint!

Some machines have an adjustable attachment for guiding parallel rows of quilting. If you have one, use that as a guide to sew the correct heading depth.

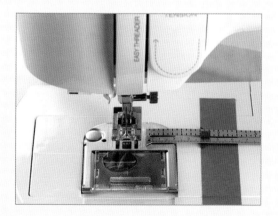

cloud valance

Made like a simple rod-pocket valance, this top treatment is cut with extra length and has four columns of rings sewn on the back. The rings in each column are tied together, which makes the fabric fall in pretty poufs at the bottom.

The Sample

- Shown in medium-weight floral-stripe cotton broadcloth
- Fullness: 1½ times the horizontal wall space (including returns)
- Finished dimensions: 75" wide × 27" long (191 × 69 cm); 16½" (42 cm) long at shortest point when rigged

Supplies

- curtain rod (shown 2½" [6.5 cm] deep with 4½" [11.5 cm] returns)
- thread
- 12 small plastic rings
- 1 yd. (1 m) of shade cord, cut in quarters
- pins
- scissors
- L-square and long straightedge
- pressing templates: 6" (16 cm) and 3" (8 cm) deep (page 36)
- fabric marker
- hand-sewing needle

Allowances

- Rod-pocket hem allowance: 6" (16 cm)
- Bottom hem allowance: 3" (8 cm)
- Joining seam allowance (if needed, add to each piece): ½" (2 cm)
- Side hem allowance (add to each vertical edge): 3" (8 cm)

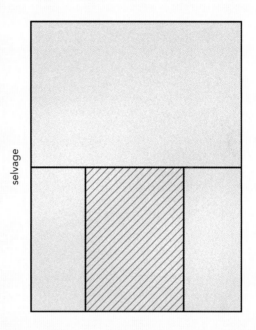

selvage

Measure, Plan, Buy Fabric

Determine the mounting style for your valance (page 14) and measure the window (page 25). Calculate the dimensions (the valance should be 11" [28 cm] longer than the finished length desired at the shortest point) and determine the yardage (page 29). Figure the cut length using the rod-pocket and bottom hem allowances. If you use a different-size curtain rod than the one indicated, plan the rod-pocket allowance to fit (page 28). Refer to the cutting layout above to help you plan.

cloud valance

1 Cut out the fabric pieces for the valance, as described on page 51. If you need to join two or more pieces of fabric to get the right width, sew them together. Press the seam allowances open.

2 Turn the valance wrong side up on your ironing board. Working with the 3" (8 cm) template, press a double hem first along the bottom and then along each side edge (page 36). The finished hems will be 1½" (4 cm) deep. Do not pin the hems to the valance body yet.

3 With the valance still wrong side up on your ironing board, unfold the pressed hems at one corner. Poke a pin through the intersection of the inside creases before you make the diagonal fold. Fold up the fabric diagonally over the protruding pin, aligning the creases in the two layers along each edge, as shown in the photo. Press the diagonal fold (use the tip of the iron along the fold only, so you keep the other creases). Remove the pin.

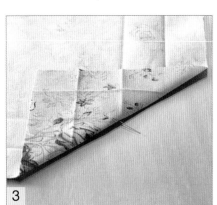

4 Refold the double hem on one edge of the corner and press it lightly.

5 Refold the double hem on the other edge of the same corner. The diagonal fold now forms a neat miter, exposing an excess square of the corner fabric peeking above the hems. Press the corner to secure all the folds. Then lift the hems and cut away the extra square of fabric.

6 Repeat steps 3, 4, and 5 at the other bottom corner. Then pin the inside crease of all three hems to the body, ready to sew. Sew a topstitched hem (page 39) as follows: Begin at the top right, sew the right hem, pivot at the corner, sew the bottom hem, pivot at the corner, and sew the left side hem.

7 Press and sew the rod pocket, as shown in the sidebar on page 45. Work with the 6" (16 cm) pressing template.

For a wider window,
add more columns of rings.

8 Sew the rings to the wrong side of the valance, as explained in the sidebar at right. Make four columns with three rows of rings: Place the outer columns 1" (2.5 cm) in from each edge, on the side hems, and space the two remaining columns evenly between them. Space the rows 7" (18 cm) apart, placing the first row ¼" (6 mm) above the bottom edge.

9 Tie the rings together, as shown in the bottom right photo in the sidebar.

10 Slide the curtain rod into the rod pocket, gathering the valance onto the rod. If the rod has returns, make sure the inside of the rod is oriented toward the wrong side of the valance. Place the rod in its brackets or inside the window if it is a tension rod.

draping a valance with rings

You can rig a valance so the lower portion falls in scalloped poufs or horizontal folds. Sew rings to the wrong side in a grid pattern—with the rings aligned at regular intervals in vertical columns and horizontal rows. Then thread a length of cord through each vertical set of rings, slide the rings together, and tie the cord to secure them. If your valance has a lot of fullness (like a cloud valance, for example), the lower edge will fall into poufs. If it has no fullness, the lower edge will fall into gently draping horizontal folds.

1. Turn the valance wrong side up. With a ruler and fabric marker or pins, measure and mark the spacing for the columns on the bottom hem. Mark the outer columns 1" (2.5 cm) in from each side edge. Divide the distance between them, as needed for your project, to find the interval for the other columns. (To figure out what number to divide by, subtract 1 from the total number of columns.)

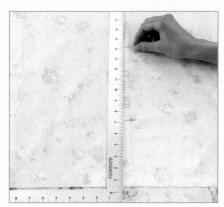

2. To mark the ring placement, align the short leg of an L-square with the bottom of the project, placing the outside of the long leg at one of the marks. Mark along the long leg of the square at whatever interval your project instructions specify for the rows. Repeat at each remaining bottom mark.

3. Neatly sew a ring to the wrong side of the valance at each mark. Align the bottom of the ring at the mark and sew over the ring several times by hand.

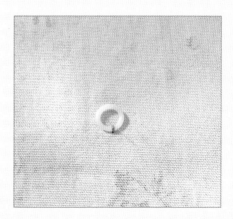

4. Thread a length of cord through the rings in one column. Slide the rings together and tie the cord to secure them. Repeat at each column.

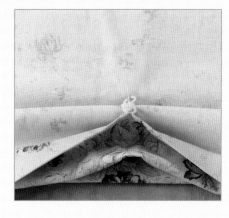

simple tie-up curtain

Ribbons tied in pretty bows cradle the pleated fabric that cascades at the sides of this top treatment. But those ribbons are just decorative—they very nicely cover the rigging that supports the shape.

The Sample

- Shown in embroidered cotton voile
- Fullness: 1 time the horizontal wall space (including returns), plus 2" (5 cm) for ease
- 52" wide by 58" long (132 × 148 cm); 27" (67 cm) long at shortest point when rigged

Supplies

- curtain rod (shown 2½" [6.5 cm] deep with 4½" [11.5 cm] returns)
- thread
- 12 small plastic rings
- 1 yd. (1 m) shade cord, cut in half
- 5 yd. (4.6 m) 1" (2.5 cm)-wide grosgrain ribbon, cut in half
- pins
- scissors
- L-square and long straightedge
- pressing templates: 6" (16 cm) and 3" (8 cm) deep (page 36)
- fabric marker
- hand-sewing needle

Allowances

- Rod-pocket hem allowance: 6" (16 cm)
- Bottom hem allowance: 3" (8 cm)
- Joining seam allowance (if needed, add to each piece): ½" (2 cm)
- Side hem allowance (add to each vertical edge): 3" (8 cm)

selvage

Measure, Plan, Buy Fabric

Determine the mounting style for your valance (page 14) and measure the window (page 25). Calculate the dimensions (the tie-up should be the length of the window) and determine the yardage (page 29). Figure the cut length using the rod-pocket and bottom hem allowances. If you use a different size curtain rod than the one indicated, plan the rod pocket allowance to fit (page 28). Refer to the cutting layout above to help you plan.

simple tie-up curtain

1 Cut out the fabric pieces for the valance, as described on page 55. If you need to join two or more pieces of fabric to get the right width, sew them together. Press open the seam allowances.

2 Turn the valance wrong side up on your ironing board. Working with the 3" (8 cm) template, press a double hem first along the bottom and then along each side edge (page 36). The finished hems will be 1½" (4 cm) deep. Do not pin the hems to the valance body yet.

3 Prepare miters at both lower corners, as explained in steps 3 through 5 of Cloud Valance, page 52.

4 Pin the inside crease of all three hems to the body, ready to sew. Sew a topstitched hem (page 39) as follows: Begin at the top right, sew the right hem, pivot at the corner, sew the bottom hem, pivot at the corner, and sew the left side hem.

5 Press and sew the rod pocket, as shown in the sidebar on page 45. Work with the 6" (16 cm) pressing template.

6 Sew the rings to the wrong side of the valance, as shown in the sidebar on page 53. Make two columns with six rows of rings: Divide the width of the valance by 4 and place the columns at that distance from each side edge. Space the rows at 7" (18 cm) intervals, placing the first row just above the bottom edge.

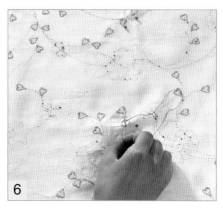

7 Tie the rings together, as shown in the bottom right photo of the sidebar on page 53.

here's a hint!

If your curtain is a different length than the project, you may need more or fewer rows of rings.

Try this design in ivory silk or even plain muslin, with matching ribbons—so sweet!

8 Slide the curtain rod into the rod pocket. If the rod has returns, make sure the inside of the rod is oriented toward the wrong side of the valance. Place the rod in its brackets or inside the window if it is a tension rod.

9 Pass one length of ribbon over the top of the valance and bring the ends together at the bottom. Position the ribbon over the tied-up pleats on one side. Tie a bow in the ribbon at the bottom, as shown in the photo below. Repeat, passing the other length of ribbon over the remaining tied-up area.

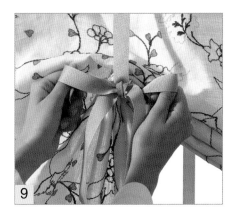

10 Cut the ends of the ribbon at an angle or in a notch if you like.

valance with belt-loop tabs

This cute valance is made from one long piece of fabric, which is turned sideways at the top of the window. It looks as though it is pleated, but it isn't. It just hangs that way when the tabs that are topstitched to the surface are pushed together on the rod. Clever!

The Sample

- Shown in striped cotton broadcloth with chenille accent stripes
- Fullness: 1¾ times the horizontal wall space
- Finished dimensions: 71½" wide by 12½" long (184 × 32 cm)

Supplies

- curtain rod (decorative type is shown, ⅜" [1 cm] in diameter)
- thread
- pins
- scissors
- ruler and long straightedge
- pressing template: 3" (8 cm) deep (page 36)
- fabric marker

Allowances

Valance
- Top hem allowance: 3" (8 cm)
- Bottom hem allowance: 3" (8 cm)
- Joining seam allowance (if needed, add to each piece): ½" (2 cm)
- Side hem allowance (add to each vertical edge): 3" (8 cm)

Tabs
- Cut enough 4" (10 cm)-wide strips to make 21 tabs, each 3" (8 cm) long. (See page 61 for tips on determining the number of tabs.)

Measure, Plan, Buy Fabric

Determine mounting style for your valance (page 14) and measure the window (page 25). Calculate the dimensions and determine the yardage (page 29), but, if you decide to turn the fabric sideways on your window as for the project shown here, use the cut width instead of the cut length to figure the yardage. Figure the cut dimensions using the hem allowances. If you use a different size curtain rod than the one indicated, adjust the tab length as needed. Refer to the cutting layout below to help you plan.

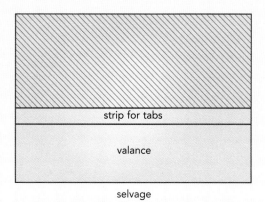

strip for tabs

valance

selvage

valance with belt-loop tabs

1 Cut out the fabric for the valance, as described on page 59. If you need to join two or more pieces of fabric to get the right width, sew them together. Press open the seam allowances.

2 Turn the valance wrong side up on your ironing board. Working with the 3" (8 cm) template, press a double hem first along the top edge, next along the bottom edge, and then along each side edge (page 36). The finished hems will be 1½" (4 cm) deep. Do not pin the hems to the valance body yet.

3 Prepare miters at all four corners, as explained in steps 3 through 5 of Cloud Valance, page 52.

4 Pin the inside crease of all four hems to the body. Sew a topstitched hem (page 39) as follows: Begin at the top right, sew the right hem, pivot at the corner, sew the bottom hem, pivot at the corner, and sew the left side hem.

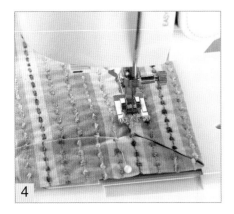

5 Sew the tabs as explained in the sidebar on the facing page. Press under ½" (2 cm) at each end of each tab (onto the side with the seam).

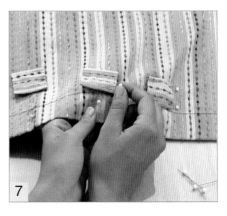

6 Lay your valance right side up on your work surface, with the top edge closest to you. Place a tab, right side up, at each side edge, aligning the tab top with the hem topstitching. Measure halfway across one of those tabs (¾" or 2 cm) and mark its midpoint with a pin placed on the topstitching line. From the pin, measure and mark 3½" (9 cm) intervals across the valance on the topstitching line.

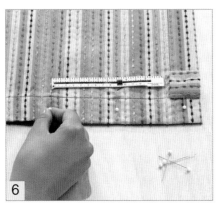

7 Pin a tab at each mark, centering the tab end on the mark. Make sure the tab is flat and pin the other end to the valance. too.

8 Sew each end of each tab to the valance: First sew all the way across the valance, securing the top end of the tabs as you go. Then sew across again, securing the bottom end.

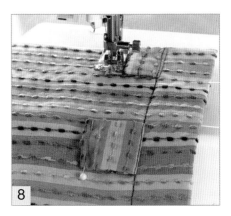

9 Slide the valance onto the curtain rod. Place the rod in its brackets, making sure that the tabs face out.

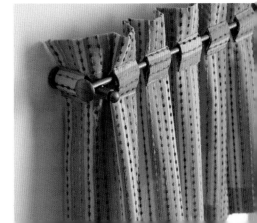

In a hurry? Attach ribbons
instead of making tabs.

determining the number of tabs

The fabric folds to the back between the tabs when this valance is hung, so the tabs must be spaced closely together. If they're far apart, there won't be room for the fabric between the rod and the window. We allowed 2" (5 cm) between the tabs, which are 1½" (4 cm) wide. This makes the total width needed for one tab and one space 3½" (9 cm).

To find the number of tabs needed, subtract 1½" (4 cm) from the finished width of your valance (for one end tab) and divide the remainder by 3½" (9 cm). Then add one tab for the end. (If you get a fraction when you divide, simply round up to the next whole number. See Tab Spacing Math on page 84.)

For example, for the valance shown:
71½" (finished width) − 1½" (one end tab) = 70"
70" ÷ 3½" (tab and space interval) = 20 tabs
20 tabs + 1 end tab = 21 tabs total
or
184 cm − 4 cm = 180 cm
180 cm ÷ 9 cm = 20 tabs
20 tabs + 1 end tab = 21 tabs total

sewing belt-loop tabs

Tabs are small pieces of fabric that are folded, sewn into a tube, turned right side out, and pressed flat. If you like, choose a fabric that contrasts the body of your project—a different color or pattern can be fun. Or, if the fabric is a stripe, turn the stripes 90 degrees when you cut the tabs. Your project instructions give you the dimensions for the tabs—but to save time, you can cut and sew the tabs as long strips, turn them right side out, and then cut the strips into individual tabs, as shown here.

1. Fold each tab (or tab strip) in half lengthwise, wrong side out. Sew the long edges together with ½" (1 cm) seam allowance, forming a tube. Rotate the seam so it is centered on the opposite side of the tube. Press the seam with only the tip of your iron so as not to crease the tube edges.

2. Turn the tube right side out. Make sure that the seam is centered as in the previous step. Press the tube flat, so the edges are creased. If you are working with a tab strip, cut the tube into pieces that are the length specified for your tabs.

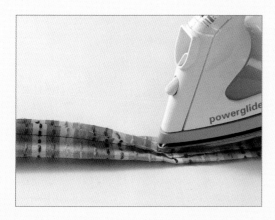
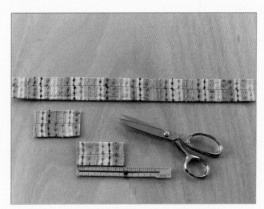

working with linings and trims

A lining gives your window treatment a clean finish that not only looks nice when viewed from outside the house but also protects your decorative fabric from sun damage. The good news is, a lined curtain or valance is just as easy to sew as an unlined one. The seams that join the two layers of fabric take the place of some or all of the hems. While the lining makes the wrong side of a curtain or valance look nice, braid, cord, or other trims make the right side look fabulous!

lined tie-up with buttoned ties

A lining gives this valance a neat finish that is speedy to sew. There are no hems to fold and press. The bias-cut ties appear to raise and support the lower edge, but the draping is controlled by rings that are sewn to the wrong side and tied together.

The Sample

- Shown in plaid silk taffeta
- Fullness: 1 time the horizontal wall space (including returns), plus 2" (5 cm) for ease
- Finished dimensions: 52" wide by 58" long (132 × 148 cm); 20" (47 cm) long at shortest point when rigged

Supplies

- curtain rod (shown 2½" [6.5 cm] deep with 4½" [11.5 cm] returns)
- 14 small plastic rings
- 1 yd. (1 m) shade cord, cut in half
- 2 buttons, about 1" (2.5 cm) in diameter
- thread
- pins
- scissors
- L-square and long straightedge
- pressing template: 6" (16 cm) deep (page 36)

Allowances

Valance face

- Rod-pocket hem allowance: 6" (16 cm)
- Bottom hem allowance (includes ½" [2 cm] for seam allowance): 3½" (10 cm)
- Joining seam allowance (if needed, add to each piece): ½" (2 cm)
- Side seam allowance (add to each vertical edge): ½" (2 cm)

Ties

- Cut 2 ties, each 5" (13 cm) wide by 44" (104 cm) long (or twice the length of the rigged valance plus 4" [10 cm]).

Lining

- Cut the lining 6" (16 cm) shorter and the same width as the valance face.

Measure, Plan, Buy Fabric

Determine the mounting style (page 14) and measure the window (page 25). Calculate the dimensions (the tie-up should be the length of the window) and determine the yardage (page 29). Figure the cut length using the rod-pocket and bottom hem allowances. If you use a different-size curtain rod than the one indicated, plan the rod-pocket allowance to fit (page 28). Refer to the cutting layout below to help you plan.

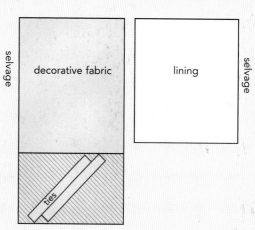

1 Cut out the decorative fabric pieces for the valance face, as described on page 65. If you need to join two or more pieces of fabric to get the right width, sew them together. Press open the seam allowances. Also cut and join the pieces for the lining.

2 Place the valance face and lining pieces right sides together, with the bottom edges aligned. Pin the bottom edges together. Sew them together with a ½" (2 cm) seam allowance.

3 Press open the seam allowances. Then press them toward the lining.

4 Fold the valance face and lining so the top edges align and the right sides are together. The hem allowance of the face fabric will fold up toward the lining. Pin the face and lining together along each side seam.

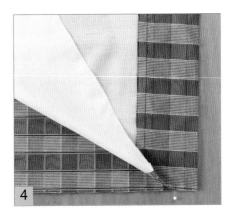

here's a hint!

To minimize the bulk in the bottom corners, cut off a small wedge of the seam allowance at the corner before you turn the valance right side out.

5 Sew the side seams with a ½" (2 cm) seam allowance. Press open the seam allowances from the top to as close to the bottom as you can. Turn the valance right side out. Press the side seams so the fabrics fold sharply along the seam.

6 Lay the valance out flat on your work surface, lining side up. Smooth the fabric and pin the layers together at the bottom along the hem/lining seam. Measure with a ruler to make sure the hem is 3" (8 cm) deep. Pin together the top edges of the face and the lining.

7 Press the hem crease. Remove the pins from the lining/hem seam as you go.

8 Sew the layers together close to the top edge.

9 Press and sew a double hem for the rod pocket, as shown in the sidebar on page 45. Work with the 6" (16 cm) pressing template and fold the two layers of fabric together as if they were one. The finished pocket will be 3" (8 cm) deep.

10 Sew the rings to the wrong side of the valance, as shown in the sidebar on page 53. Make two columns with seven rows of rings, as follows: Divide the width of the valance by 4 and place the columns at that distance from each side edge. Space the rows at 7" (18 cm) intervals, placing the first row just above the bottom edge.

11 Tie the rings together as shown in the sidebar on page 53.

12 Fold one tie in half lengthwise, wrong side out. Pin the long edges together. With a ½" (1 cm) seam allowance, sew across one end, pivot at the corner, and sew about halfway down the long edge. Backstitch. Leave a 4" (10 cm) space and then continue the seam along the remainder of the long edge and across the other end. Repeat to make the other tie.

13 Trim the seam allowance at the corners of each tie.

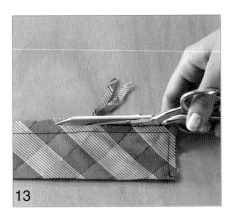

Want to get fancy?
Make covered buttons and
loop a pretty tassel over each one.

14 Turn each tie right side out through the opening.

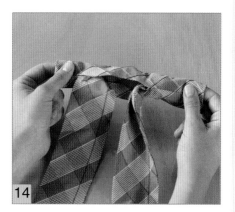

15 Press the ties, folding the fabric sharply along the seamed edges. Sew the openings closed by hand or topstitch them close to the edge.

16 Make buttonholes in one end of each tie and sew a button to the other end, as explained in the sidebar below. Begin the buttonhole 1" (2.5 cm) from the tie end. Mark for the center of the button 1¼" (4.5 cm) from the opposite end of the tie.

17 Slide the curtain rod into the rod pocket. If the rod has returns, make sure the inside of the rod is oriented toward the wrong side of the valance. Place the rod in its brackets or inside the window if it is a tension rod.

tips for sewing buttonholes and buttons

The buttonhole on a tie should be perpendicular to the tie's end. When the tie is fastened, the weight of the button will pull the hole closed. Each project in this book provides instruction for the placement of any buttonholes and buttons, but here are some tips in case you have a button of a different size.

Planning

• The buttonhole must be a little larger than the diameter of the button. Usually, it needs to be about ⅛" (2 mm) larger. Make a test buttonhole in scrap fabric.

• The buttonhole must be positioned so that the distance between the buttonhole end and the tie end is slightly greater than the radius of the button. The button is then framed by the tie end.

• The button must be positioned so that the distance between the button center and the tie end is greater than the buttonhole length. The buttonhole end of the tie will then completely overlap the end with the button. It looks sloppy if you can see through the buttonhole.

Sewing

Refer to your sewing machine manual for how to mark and sew the buttonhole. Mark the position of the button center on the right side of the tie. Sew on the button with a double strand of thread. Begin by inserting the needle from the wrong side of the tie so that the thread knot will be on the back. Place a toothpick on top of the button, between the holes, and pass the thread over it as you sew. The gap created by the toothpick will make the button a little bit loose and will create a shank that will accommodate the thickness of the fabric when the tie is buttoned.

Sew three or four times through the button and knot the thread on the wrong side of the tie. Cut the excess thread and remove the toothpick.

ruffled cloud valance

Dress up a cloud valance by adding a ruffle at the lower edge to compliment the heading at the top. A lining hides the top edge of the ruffle and finishes the valance sides and lower edge at the same time. The only hem to fold and press is for the rod pocket.

The Sample

- Shown in medium-weight floral-print cotton, with polka-dot print for the ruffle
- Fullness: 1½ times the horizontal wall space (including returns)
- Ruffle fullness: 1½ times the finished width of valance
- Finished dimensions: 75" wide by 32" long (191 × 81 cm); 21½" (54 cm) long at shortest point when rigged

Supplies

- curtain rod (shown 2½" [6.5 cm] deep with 4½" [11.5 cm] returns)
- 12 small plastic rings
- 2 yd. (1.8 m) of shade cord or cable cord, cut in quarters
- thread: sewing thread and button thread
- pins
- scissors
- L-square and long straightedge
- pressing template: 10" (25.5 cm) deep (page 36)

Allowances

Valance face
- Rod-pocket hem allowance: 10" (26 cm)
- Bottom hem allowance: ½" (2 cm)
- Joining seam allowance (if needed, add to each piece): ½" (2 cm)
- Side seam allowance (add to each vertical edge): ½" (2 cm)

Lining
- Cut the lining the same size as the valance face.

Ruffle

- Cut enough 7" (19 cm) long strips to give you the desired fullness for your fabric. (See the sidebar on page 71 for tips on planning a ruffle.)

Measure, Plan, Buy Fabric

Determine the mounting style (page 14) and measure the window (page 25). Calculate the valance dimensions and determine the yardage (page 29). Figure the cut length using the rod-pocket and bottom hem allowances. If you use a different-size curtain rod than the one indicated, plan the rod-pocket allowance to fit (page 28). Refer to the cutting layout below to help you plan.

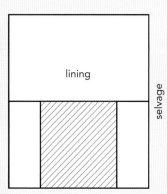

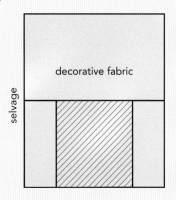

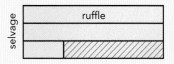

ruffled cloud valance

1 Cut out the decorative fabric pieces for the valance face, as described in the box on page 69. If you need to join two or more pieces of fabric to get the right width, sew them together. Press open the seam allowances. Also cut and join the pieces for the lining and the strips for the ruffles.

2 Fold the ruffle in half, wrong side out, bringing together the long edges. Pin the layers together at each end. Sew across each end with a ½" (2 cm) seam allowance. Turn the ends right side out. Press, creasing the fabric sharply along the seams.

3 Now fold the ruffle in half again, this time right side out, bringing the long edges together. Press the folded edge.

4 Fold the ruffle crosswise in half and mark the fold with a safety pin or fabric marker.

5 Place the ruffle in the bed of your sewing machine, with one end under the presser foot and the long cut edge aligned with the ⅛" (5 mm) seam guide on the throat plate. Set the machine to a wide, long zigzag stitch. Place the spool of button thread on the auxiliary spool pin.

6 To prepare the ruffle for gathering, pull the end of the button thread and place it on the ruffle, under the foot, letting a 6" (15 cm) tail of thread extend behind the foot. Zigzag-stitch over the thread, unspooling more thread as you go and being careful not to catch the thread in the stitches. With your right index finger, guide the button thread into position on top of the ruffle as you sew.

7 When you reach the halfway mark, stop sewing, lift the presser foot, and pull 12" (30 cm) of button thread past the needle. Lower the presser foot and continue to the end. At the end, cut the button thread, leaving a 6" (15 cm) tail.

8 Lay the ruffle on your work surface. Insert a pin across the zigzag stitching at each end. Wrap the tail of button thread in a figure eight around the pin. You can see the figure eight in photo ten.

9 Find the 12" (30 cm) loop of button thread halfway across the ruffle. Cut the loop in half. Gently pull one of the thread ends, pushing the fabric toward the pin at the ruffle end and gathering it on the thread. Do the same with the other thread end.

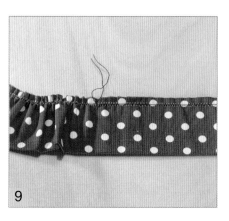

10 Lay the valance on your work surface, right side up, with the bottom edge toward you. Mark the bottom edge ¼" (2.5 cm) in from each side edge and also at the midpoint. Lay the ruffle on top of it, with the side with the button-thread tails face up. Position the fold away from you and align the gathered edge with the bottom edge of the valance. Pin the ends of the ruffle to the valance at the side marks. Pin the midpoints together, too.

11 Adjust the gathers so that the ruffle is evenly gathered and lies flat across the valance. Unwrap the thread tails in the middle if you need to make the gathering looser or tighter. Pin the ruffle to the valance. Tie together the button-thread tails in the middle. Sew the ruffle to the valance, stitching once with a ½" (2 cm) seam allowance and again with a ¼" (1 cm) seam allowance.

12 Lay the valance right side up on your work surface, with the ruffle on the valance as before. Lay the lining wrong side up on top of the valance, aligning all the edges. Pin the layers together along the sides and bottom. Sew together with a ½" (2 cm) seam allowance, starting at one top corner, sewing down one side edge, across the bottom, and up the other side edge.

Ruffles are fun in a matching fabric, too.

13 Trim the bottom corners and turn the valance right side out. Press, folding the fabric sharply along the seamed edges and folding the ruffle down, away from the valance.

14 Lay the valance flat and pin the face fabric and lining together along the top. Sew the layers together close to the top edge.

15 Press and sew a double hem for the rod pocket and heading, as shown in the sidebar on page 45. Work with the 10" (26 cm) pressing template and fold the two layers of fabric together as if they were one. The heading depth is 2" (5 cm).

16 Sew the rings to the wrong side of the valance, as shown in the sidebar on page 53. Make four columns with three rows of rings. Place the outer columns 1" (2 cm) in from each edge and space the two remaining columns evenly between them. Space the rows at 7" (18 cm) intervals, placing the first row right above the ruffle.

17 Slide the curtain rod into the rod pocket, gathering the valance onto the rod. If the rod has returns, make sure the inside of the rod is oriented toward the wrong side of the valance. Place the rod in its brackets or inside the window if it is a tension rod.

planning a ruffle

The easiest way to make a ruffle is by folding a strip of fabric in half so that the fold becomes the ruffle hem. The cut edges are gathered together and sewn into the seam between the face fabric and lining.

The amount of gathering is the fullness (page 27). You can make the ruffle as full as you like, but if the main portion of your project also has fullness, it's best to use the same ratio for the ruffle.

The length is the top-to-bottom dimension (from gathers to hem). The width is the side-to-side dimension. So, the ruffle length is much shorter than the width! You can lay out ruffle strips lengthwise or crosswise on your fabric.

scalloped valance with trim

The scalloped hemline gives this valance a soft, pretty finish. The valance and lining are cut exactly the same size and shape. You sew them together along all the edges except the top. Then turn them right side out. How easy! Add tassel fringe for an elegant finish.

The Sample

- Shown in medium-weight cotton woven with heavier ribbon stripes
- Fullness: 1½ times the horizontal wall space (including returns)
- Finished dimensions: 75" wide × 18" long (191 × 46 cm)

Supplies

- curtain rod (shown 2½" [6.5 cm] deep with 4½" [11.5 cm] returns)
- tassel fringe, enough to cover scalloped edge of valance plus 6" (15 cm)
- thread
- pins
- scissors
- L-square and long straightedge
- pattern paper or muslin
- pressing template: 10" (26 cm) deep (page 36)

Allowances

Valance face

- Rod-pocket hem allowance: 10" (26 cm)
- Bottom hem allowance: ½" (2 cm)
- Joining seam allowance (if needed, add to each piece): ½" (2 cm)

- Side-seam allowance (add to each vertical edge): ½" (2 cm)

Lining

- Cut the lining the same size as the valance face.

Measure, Plan, Buy Fabric

Determine the mounting style for your valance (page 14) and measure the window (page 25). Calculate the valance dimensions and determine the yardage (page 29). Figure the cut length using the rod-pocket and bottom hem allowances. If you use a different-size curtain rod than the one indicated, plan the rod-pocket allowance to fit (page 28). Refer to the cutting layout below to help you plan.

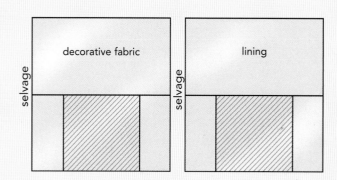

scalloped valance with trim

1 As explained on page 33, make a half-pattern for your valance. Set aside your pattern.

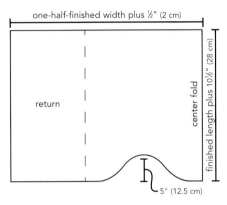

one-half-finished width plus ½" (2 cm)

return

center fold

finished length plus 10½" (28 cm)

5" (12.5 cm)

Scalloped valance half-pattern

2 Cut out the decorative fabric pieces for the valance face, as described on page 73. Cut the pieces to the greatest length needed, without shaping the lower edge. If you need to join two or more pieces of fabric to get the right width, sew them together. Press open the seam allowances. Also cut and join the pieces for the lining.

3 Fold the joined decorative fabric in half along its vertical center. Place your half-pattern on top, aligning the center fold, side, and top edges. Cut the bottom edge. Cut the lining in the same way.

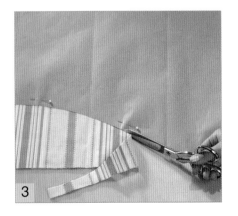

4 Pin the lining to the decorative fabric, right sides together, aligning all the edges. Sew together with a ½" (2 cm) seam allowance, starting at one top corner, sewing down one side edge, across the bottom, and up the other side edge.

5 Diagonally trim the bottom corners. Clip the seam allowance on the inside curves and notch it on the outside curves.

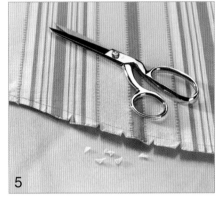

6 Turn the valance right side out. Press, folding the fabric sharply along the seamed edges. Lay the valance flat and pin the face fabric and lining together along the top. Sew the layers together close to the top edge.

Line eyelet fabric with a cheery color that will peek through.

7 Press and sew a double hem for the rod pocket and heading, as explained in the sidebar on page 49. Work with the 10" (26 cm) pressing template and fold the two layers of fabric together as if they were one. The heading depth is 2" (5 cm).

8 Pin and then sew the trim to the scalloped edge of the valance, as shown in the sidebar on the facing page.

9 Slide the curtain rod into the rod pocket, gathering the valance onto the rod. If the rod has returns, make sure the inside of the rod is oriented toward the wrong side of the valance. Place the rod in its brackets or inside the window if it is a tension rod.

here's a hint!

If your trim is too thick to turn under, cut it flush with the vertical edge of the valance and zigzag-stitch the ends so they don't fray.

fitting and sewing trim

Braid, fringe, ribbon, and other trims look pretty when sewn to a curved edge—but unless they are eased to follow the contour, they will buckle and cause the fabric to pucker.

1. Lay the valance flat, right side up on your work surface, with the curved edge closest to you. Lay the trim right side up on top of the curve and decide how far above the edge to place it. For fringed trim, the fringe usually extends below the fabric and the braid sits on top of the fabric, right at the edge. You can place other types of trims at whatever distance from the edge that you like. It's easiest to place trim right at the edge, because then you don't need to measure and mark a guideline.

2. Position the trim so it extends about 3" (8 cm) beyond the right-hand vertical edge of the valance, as shown below. Pin it to the valance about 1" (2.5 cm) in from the vertical edge.

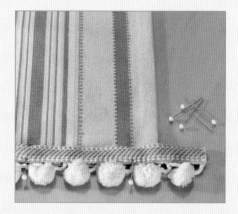

3. Lay the trim smoothly along the edge of the valance, but don't stretch it. Pin it every 4" to 5" (10 to 13 cm). As you pin the area where the valance edge curves toward you, keep the bottom edge of the trim flat as it follows the curve. As you sew, the top edge will be eased

onto the fabric to lie smoothly on the smaller inside curve. Pin every couple of inches (centimeters), as shown below.

4. As you pin the area where the valance edge curves away from you, keep the top edge of the trim flat as it follows the curve, as shown below. Let the bottom edge be looser (but make sure the trim stays parallel to the valance edge). Pin every couple of inches (centimeters).

5. When you reach the left-hand vertical edge of the valance, let the trim extend off the edge for at least 3"

(8 cm), just in case you need to adjust it. Press the lower edge of the valance to help the pinned trim follow the contoured edge.

6. Sew the top edge of trim to the valance, starting about 1" (2 cm) in from the right-hand vertical edge. Pull out the pins as you go and stop stitching about 1" (2 cm) before the left-hand edge. If you wish, sew the bottom edge of the trim, starting and stopping in the same way. (Some trims will require you to sew the bottom edge. This project has only the top edge sewn on.) Press the curved edge again to make sure it's smooth.

7. Cut each end of the trim so it extends about ½" (1.5 cm). Tuck the end between the trim and the fabric. Sew the end of the trim to the valance. Sew toward the end of the trim along its top and then the bottom edges, instead of starting at the end and sewing toward the center.

pointed valance with cord-and-tassel trim

This valance—cut to lie flat across the window—has a simple elegance. The effect is enhanced by decorator cord and a tassel hanging from the center point on the lower edge. Because the valance has no fullness, you'll most likely be able to make it from a single length of fabric.

The Sample
- Shown in embroidered, medium-weight, silk
- Fullness: 1 time the horizontal wall space (including returns), plus 1" (3 cm) for ease
- Finished dimensions: 52" wide × 22" long (132 × 56 cm)

Supplies
- curtain rod (shown 2½" [6.5 cm] deep with 4½" [11.5 cm] returns)
- decorator cord, enough to cover lower edge of valance plus 6" (15 cm)
- decorator tassel
- thread
- pins
- scissors
- L-square and long straightedge
- flexible ruler (optional)
- pattern paper or muslin
- pressing template: 6" (16 cm) deep (page 36)

Allowances
Valance face
- Rod-pocket hem allowance: 6" (16 cm)
- Bottom hem allowance: ½" (2 cm)
- Side seam allowance (add to each vertical edge): ½" (2 cm)

Lining
- Cut the lining the same size as the valance face.

selvage | decorative fabric | lining | selvage

Measure, Plan, Buy Fabric
Determine the mounting style (page 14) and measure the window (page 25). Calculate the valance dimensions and determine the yardage (page 29). Figure the cut length using the rod-pocket and bottom hem allowances. If you use a different-size curtain rod than the one indicated, plan the rod-pocket allowance to fit (page 28). Refer to the cutting layout above to help you plan.

pointed valance with cord-and-tassel trim

1   Make a half-pattern for your valance, as explained in steps 1, 2, and 5 of Preparing Shaped Hemlines on page 33. Begin with a horizontal top line equal to half the horizontal wall space, plus the return depth, plus ½" (1.5 cm) for ease.

one-half finished width plus ½" (2 cm)

return

center fold

finished length plus 6½" (18 cm)

7" (17.5 cm)

Pointed valance half-pattern

2   Fold the decorative fabric in half lengthwise. Place the pattern on it, aligning the center fold and top edges. Cut out the valance. Cut the lining in the same way.

3   Sew the cord to the lower edge of the decorative fabric, as explained on the facing page. Lay the tassel on the decorative fabric at the center point. Position it so the hanging loop extends

off the fabric and the tassel knot lies on the fabric just above the decorative cord. Sew over the hanging loop close to the decorative cord.

4   Pin the lining to the decorative fabric, right sides together, aligning all the edges. Sew together with a ½" (2 cm) seam allowance, starting at one top corner, sewing down one side edge, across the bottom, and up the other side edge. Attach the zipper foot to sew the bottom edge.

5   Sew over the hanging loop in the point's seam allowance again, so the tassel won't gradually slip below the point.

5

6   Turn the valance right side out. The decorator cord will extend along the bottom edge. Press, folding the fabric sharply along the seamed edges and taking care not to crush the cord.

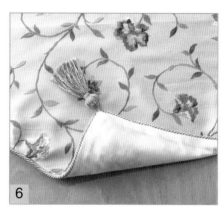

6

7   Press and sew a double hem for the rod pocket, as explained in the sidebar on page 45. Work with the 6" (16 cm) pressing template and fold the two layers of fabric together as if they were one. The finished pocket will be 3" (8 cm) deep.

8   Slide the curtain rod into the rod pocket. If the rod has returns, make sure the inside of the rod is oriented toward the wrong side of the valance. Place the rod in its brackets or inside the window if it is a tension rod.

3

For a tassel with a cord medallion, sew the medallion to the face of the finished valance.

attaching decorator cord

Decorator cord adds a sophisticated finishing touch. If you want to apply cord at the edge of a project, choose the type that is attached to a flat tape so you can sew it into the edge seam. You don't have to pin the cord to your project before sewing—it's usually easier to handle if you don't.

1. Put the cording foot or zipper foot on your sewing machine. Place the project right side up on the bed of the machine. Lay the cord on top of the fabric, with the cord to the left of the needle and the tape even with the cut edge of the seam allowance. Insert the needle close to the cord, lower the presser foot, and sew. The tape should lie smoothly on the fabric.

3. With the needle still down, rotate the project, so you're ready to sew the adjacent edge. Swing the tape around the corner or point, aligning it with the cut edge of the seam allowance as before. Lower the presser foot and continue. The cord will bunch up inside the point—that's okay, but it will feel awkward to sew around. Continue to sew as before.

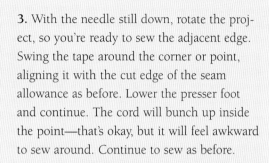

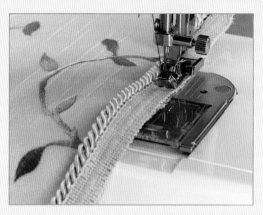

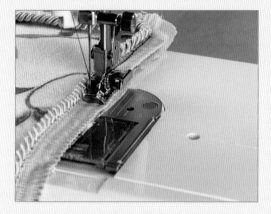

2. Continue to sew, feeding the fabric and tape evenly under the foot with your fingers. If you want to turn a corner or sew around a point, stitch exactly to the point where the seamline turns the corner. Stop stitching with your needle down. Raise the presser foot and, with small pointed scissors, clip the tape almost up to the cord.

4. To sew the cord to a curve, keep the cord itself smooth along the seamline. The tape may flute a little on an inside curve or need to be stretched to flare around an outside curve. Many tapes ravel easily, so try to avoid clipping the tape on curves—but you may have to in order for the tape to follow an outside curve or lie flat when the piece is lined. Apply a seam sealant to keep the clipped tape from raveling.

lined panels with tabs and tiebacks

These curtain panels look pleated when they're open—thanks to the hidden tabs, which fold to the back and slide along the rod. If you are making a pair of curtains, be sure to buy and cut enough fabric for two panels. Complete each step on both panels as you go, instead of completing one panel at a time.

The Sample
- Shown in medium-weight printed linen
- Fullness: 2 times the horizontal wall space
- Finished dimension of each panel: 49" wide x 88" long (125 × 213 cm)

Supplies
- curtain rod (decorative type is shown)
- thread
- curtain weights (2 per panel)
- 4 small plastic rings (for tiebacks)
- pins
- scissors
- L-square and long straightedge
- pressing templates: 5" (13 cm) and 2" (5 cm) deep (page 36)

Allowances
Outer panel
- Top allowance: ½" (2 cm)
- Bottom-hem allowance: 5" (13 cm)
- Joining seam allowance (if needed to join widths, add to each piece): ½" (2 cm)
- Side hem allowance (add to each vertical edge): 2" (5 cm)

Tabs
- Cut 9 tabs 4" wide × 4½" long (10 × 14 cm).

Tiebacks
- Cut each 28" wide x 6" long (71 × 15 cm).

Top facing
- Cut one piece 4½" (12 cm) deep and the same width as the lining.

Lining
- Cut the lining 6" (12 cm) narrower and 5" (13 cm) shorter than the outer panel.

Measure, Plan, Buy Fabric

Calculate your panel dimensions and determine the yardage (page 29). Include the allowances listed here in your dimensions. These cutting instructions are for only one panel. Refer to the cutting layout below to help you plan.

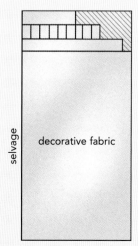
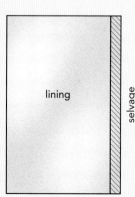

selvage   decorative fabric   lining   selvage

1 Cut out the decorative fabric pieces for the panel, as described on page 81. If you need to join two or more pieces of fabric to get the right width, sew them together with a ½" (2 cm) seam allowance. Press open the seam allowances. Cut and join the pieces for the lining.

2 Working with the 5" (13 cm) template, press a double hem at the bottom of the decorative fabric panel (page 36)—the finished hem will be 2½" (6.5 cm) deep. Pin the hem so it's ready to blind-stitch by machine. Select the blindstitch setting on your machine and sew the hem, as explained in the sidebar on the facing page. Hem the bottom of the lining panel in the same way.

3 Pin the long edge of the top facing to the top of the lining panel, with right sides together. Sew the pieces with ½" (2 cm) seam allowance. Press the seam allowances toward the facing.

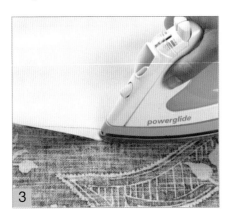

4 Sew, turn, and press each tab (page 61).

5 Working with the 2" (5 cm) template as a guide, fold and press 2" (5 cm) to the wrong side along both side edges of the decorative panel. Then lay the decorative fabric panel right side up, with the top edge closest to you, and unfold the fabric at the sides.

Measure and mark the position for the center of each tab on the top edge of the panel, as explained in the sidebar on page 83. To find the center of each end tab, measure from the fold at the side.

6 Center a tab, right side down, on each mark. Align the open end of the tab with the edge of the panel and pin. Sew each tab to the top of the panel with a ½" (2 cm) seam allowance.

here's a hint!

Place the end tabs about ⅛" (3 mm) away from the side folds to make the next steps easier and neater.

7 Lay the decorative fabric panel right side up on your work surface. Lay the lining wrong side down on top of it. Align the top edges and long (vertical) edges on one side. Pin together the long edges.

8 Shift the fabrics to align the loose long edges of the lining and decorative fabric. Pin together the edges. The panels now form a tube. Sew the pinned edges with a ½" (2 cm) seam allowance. Press the seam allowances toward the lining.

9 Lay the panel flat on your work surface, with the lining on top. Adjust the layers so the side creases are at each edge (gently refold the creases at the top). There should be an equal amount of decorative fabric next to the lining on each long edge. Pin the layers together along the top edges.

blindstitching a hem

1. To prepare a blindstitched hem, press the fabric as you would for a double or single hem, according to the project instructions or your preference (pages 36–38).

2. Don't pin the loose edge of the hem allowance to the body of the project. Instead, with the project still lying on your work surface, fold the hem under,

arranging it so a narrow margin of the hem allowance extends beyond the project, as shown in the photo at left. Gently smooth the project body along the fold. Pin through all layers, placing the pinheads toward the extending hem allowance.

3. Refer to your manual to set your sewing machine to blindstitch. Put the blindstitch foot on the machine. Place your project under the foot, aligning the fold with the guide on the foot, as shown in the photo at right. Sew. The needle will straight-stitch along the extending hem for several stitches and then zigzag to the left to make one stitch through the fold.

4. When you unfold the fabric, the single stitches will hardly show on the right side of the project. Sew a test on a scrap to see how this stitch works. Adjust the setting if needed.

making tiebacks

A tieback is like a sash that holds a curtain panel off the window. It's just a long piece of fabric with small rings sewn to the ends. Wrap the tieback around the panel and slip the rings into a cup hook in the wall.

1. To sew a tieback, fold the fabric in half lengthwise, wrong side out. With a ½" (2 cm) seam allowance, sew about halfway down the long edge and backstitch. Leave a 4" (10 cm) space and then continue the seam along the remainder of the long edge.

2. Rotate the seam so it is centered on the tube you've just sewn and sew across each end. Trim the seam allowance at the ends. Press the long seam allowances open and turn the tieback right side out through the opening.

3. Press. Sew a small ring about ½" (1.5 cm) from each end, positioned on the seam.

spacing tabs

There's really only one rule for positioning tabs at the top of curtain or valance. You need a tab at, or very close to, each end of the top edge of the curtain or valance. These tabs ensure that the side edges hang straight.

The instructions for the tabbed projects in this book specify the number of tabs shown in the project photograph, but you can have as many tabs as you like. The number of tabs will help create different effects, depending on the weight of the fabric, the fullness of the treatment, and the space between the tabs.

• If the treatment has no fullness, it will hang taut between the tabs.

• If the treatment is full, the fabric will hang in folds between the tabs. The greater the distance between the tabs, the deeper the folds will be.

• If the fabric is soft or lightweight, or the tabs are very widely spaced, the top edge of the treatment may sag between the tabs. This effect can look very nice or very sloppy, depending on your fabric and your taste.

• The width of all the tabs added together should not be greater than the width of the curtain rod. If it is, the tabs will be crushed together on the rod and the gathered fabric between them will be difficult to control.

As a rule of thumb, place a tab every 8" to 12" (20 to 30 cm).

Tab Spacing Math

To find the correct spacing for the tabs, subtract the width of one tab from the width of the top edge of the project. Divide the remaining top width by one less than the total number of tabs. For example, for a valance 62" (155 cm) wide with seven tabs that are 2" (5 cm) wide:

62" (top edge) − 2" (tab width) = 60" (remaining top edge)
60" ÷ 6 tabs = 10" tab spacing interval
or
155 cm − 5 cm = 150 cm
150 cm ÷ 6 tabs = 25-cm tab spacing interval

Remember, this interval is the distance from the center of one tab to the center of the next one. When you measure and mark the placement of the tabs for your project, first measure half the tab width from the side seamline at each end of the top (1" [2.5 cm] in our example). Then measure the distance of the interval from that point (10" [25 cm] in our example).

If you think the tab-spacing interval is too large, add a tab and do the math again. If you think the interval is too small, subtract a tab and do the math again. Be sure to sew all the tabs you plan to use.

10 Sew the pinned edges with a ½" (2 cm) seam allowance. Trim the seam allowance at the top corners. Turn the panel right side out. Press the top edge. If necessary, re-press the side creases, too.

11 Lay the panel flat with the lining up. Fold over each tab so it lies flat against the facing. Turn under ½" (2 cm) at the end of the tab and pin it to the panel.

12 Transfer the panel to your sewing machine bed, lining side up. Sew through all layers along the bottom of the facing, catching the tabs in the seams.

13 At each bottom corner of the panel, sew a weight to the inside of the side facing to help the curtains hang evenly (page 104).

14 Make a tieback for each panel, as shown in the sidebar on page 83.

15 Slide the panels onto the curtain pole. Place the pole in its brackets, making sure that the curtain lining is toward the window. Add the tiebacks.

Make another set in sheer fabric and hang them inside these for a dressier look.

adding pleats and designer details

Looking for something a little extra special? Instead of gathering your window treatment onto the rod, you can pleat it. To add interest and drama, you can incorporate one or more decorative fabrics in the design and work with layered and bordered effects. The sophisticated projects in this chapter take a bit longer to sew than those in other chapters—but they're fun to make and will add panache to your décor.

pleated tailored valance

The rod pocket for this valance is cut separately and sewn in place after the "skirt" is lined and pleated, so the fabric stays smooth over the rod, even above the pleat. Make the pleat from a contrasting or matching project. You have lots of choices!

The Sample

- Shown in medium-weight, dot-pattern jacquard. The pleat is made with the wrong side of the fabric.
- Fullness: 1 time the horizontal wall space (including returns), plus 1" (3 cm) for ease, excluding hidden part of the pleat
- Finished dimensions: 51" wide × 17½" long (130 × 45 cm), excluding the hidden part of the pleat.

Supplies

- curtain rod (shown 2½" [6.5 cm] deep with 4½" [11.5 cm] returns)
- thread
- pins
- scissors
- L-square and long straightedge
- flexible ruler (optional)
- pattern paper or muslin

Cutting List

Valance skirt face and lining
- Cut one piece from each fabric.

Pleat face and lining
- Cut one piece from each fabric.

Rod pocket
- Cut one piece 7" (19 cm) long and the width of the finished pleated valance plus 3" (8 cm)—remember your fabric is folded in half. You don't need a lining.

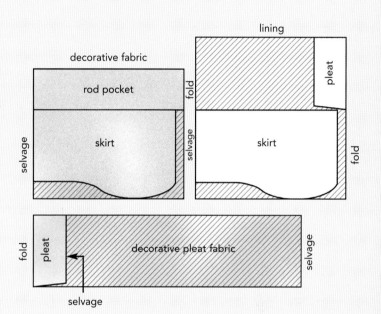

Measure, Plan, Buy Fabric

Determine the mounting style (page 14) and measure the window (page 25). Calculate your valance dimensions. Refer to steps 1 and 2 on page 90 and the cutting layout above to help you plan. Determine the yardage (page 29). When you are ready to cut out the pieces, fold the fabrics in half lengthwise and use the patterns as a guide.

pleated tailored valance

1 Make a half-pattern for your valance skirt, as explained in steps 1 and 2 of Preparing Shaped Hemline on page 33. Begin with a horizontal top line equal to half the horizontal wall width plus the return depth, plus 1" (3.5 cm) for ease and seam allowance. Make the skirt 2" (5 cm) shorter than the overall finished length to allow for the separate rod pocket and seam allowance.

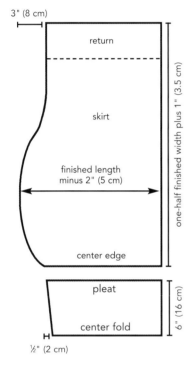

3" (8 cm)

return

skirt

one-half finished width plus 1" (3.5 cm)

finished length
minus 2" (5 cm)

center edge

pleat

center fold

6" (16 cm)

½" (2 cm)

Pleated tailored valance half-pattern

here's a hint!

Make the half-pattern ½" (1.5 cm) longer than the desired finished length and test it on your window. When you have the shape you want, shorten the pattern from the top so that it is 2" (5 cm) shorter than the desired finished length.

2 Make a 6" (16 cm)-wide half-pattern for the pleat, as shown at left. Make the side edge the same length as the center edge of the skirt pattern. Make the center fold edge ½" (2 cm) shorter than the side. Draw a curve at the bottom to connect the side and center. Mark ½" (2 cm) from the center fold on top of pattern. This pattern includes a ½" (1.5 cm) seam allowance on the top, bottom, and side edge.

3 Fold the fabric in half lengthwise and cut out the pieces as shown in the diagram at left. Transfer the mark on the top edge of the pleat pattern to both layers of one of the pleat pieces.

4 Working with the decorative fabric and a ½" (2 cm) seam allowance, pin and sew the center edge of each skirt to the corresponding side edge of the pleat. Press open the seam allowances.

5 Pin and sew the lining skirts and the pleat interior together in the same way.

6 Pin the lining skirt to the decorative fabric skirt, right sides together, aligning all the edges. Sew together with a ½" (2 cm) seam allowance, starting at one top corner, sewing down one side edge, across the bottom, and up the other side edge.

7 Clip the seam allowance along the curves (page 39). Turn the skirt right side out. Press, folding the fabric sharply along the seamed edges. Pin the top edges together along the main pieces, leaving the top of the pleat open.

8 Lay the skirt on your work surface, with decorative fabric face up. Find the marks at the top of the pleat. Pin the layers together at each mark. To form the pleat, fold the skirt along the seams (between pleat interior and skirt), aligning each seam with the closest pin mark. Pin through all layers to secure the fold.

9 Sew the top edge of the skirt closed with a long stitch and a ⅜" (1 cm) seam allowance. Gently press the pleat edges.

10 Serge or zigzag-stitch one long edge (the top edge) of the rod pocket so it won't ravel later. Fold and press the rod pocket in half, right side out, aligning the long edges.

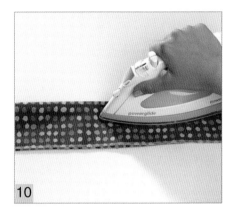
10

11 With the right sides together, pin and then sew the raw edge of the rod pocket to the top edge of the skirt. Center the rod pocket so it extends equally at each side of the skirt. Press the seam allowances toward the rod pocket.

12 Press and then sew a double hem at each end of the rod pocket (page 45), folding the extending fabric even with the sides of the skirt and covering the intersecting seam allowance. You can make a template to press the fabric over, but you don't need to—just make sure you fold the pocket end evenly.

12

13 Lay the valance right side up. Fold the rod pocket to the wrong side along the top crease. Pin through all layers from the right side. Orient the heads of the pins toward the fold. Turn the valance over to make sure the pocket stays flat.

14 Place the valance right side up in the bed of your machine, with the rod pocket just to the right of the needle. Stitch in the ditch of the previous seam to secure the back of the rod pocket to the valance. If your fabric is thick, attach the zipper foot.

14

15 Slide the curtain rod into the rod pocket. If the rod has returns, make sure the inside of the rod is oriented toward the wrong side of the valance. Place the rod in its brackets or inside the window if it is a tension rod.

It's so easy to make a contrast pleat, next time, accent the valance with two or three.

balloon valance

This balloon valance is lined, pleated, and then sewn to a separate rod pocket. Rings that are sewn to the back of the pleats and then tied together cause the fabric to drape and the pleats to fall open, creating pretty, puffy scallops.

The Sample

- Shown in medium-weight printed linen
- Fullness: 1 time the horizontal wall space (including returns), plus 1" (3 cm) for ease, plus 36" (90 cm) for three sets of pleats (12" [30 cm] for each set)
- Finished dimensions: 51" wide × 30" long (129 × 76 cm), excluding the pleats (87" [219 cm] wide before pleating); 19½" (49 cm) long at shortest point when rigged

Supplies

- curtain rod (shown 2½" [6.5 cm] deep with 4½" [11.5 cm] returns)
- thread
- 12 small plastic rings
- 1 yd. (1 m) shade cord, cut in quarters
- pins; scissors
- L-square and long straightedge
- card stock for pleating template: the width of your pouf plus 20" (51 cm) × 6" (15 cm) deep
- fabric marker
- hand-sewing needle

Cutting List

Valance face
- Top seam allowance: ½" (2 cm)
- Bottom hem allowance: (includes ½" [2 cm] for seam allowance): 3½" (10 cm)
- Joining seam allowance (if needed, add to each piece): ½" (2 cm)

- Side seam allowance (add to each vertical edge): ½" (2 cm)

Rod pocket
- Cut one piece 7" (19 cm) long and the width of the finished pleated valance plus 3" (8 cm).

Lining
- Cut the lining 6" (16 cm) shorter than and the same width as the valance face (before pleating).

Measure, Plan, Buy Fabric

Determine the mounting style (page 14) and measure the window (page 25). Calculate your valance dimensions. Refer to Planning a Balloon Valance on page 94 to see how wide to cut each piece of fabric. Figure the finished length and then subtract 3" (8 cm) to allow for the separate rod pocket. Add the hem and seam allowances noted. Determine the yardage (page 29). Refer to the cutting layout below to help you plan.

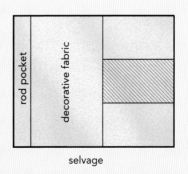
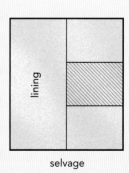

balloon valance

1 Cut out the decorative fabric pieces for the valance, as described on page 93. Sew the pieces together as planned, with a ½" (2 cm) seam allowance. Cut and join the pieces for the lining. Press open all the seam allowances.

2 Complete steps 2 through 8 of Lined Tie-up with Buttoned Ties on page 66.

3 From card stock, make a template for marking the pleats. Refer to your planning sketch. On one long edge of the template, measure and mark the single-pleat space, the pouf space, and the double-pleat space. Measure and mark the middle of the double-pleat space, too. Cut a notch at each mark. Label each space. Turn over the template and label the spaces on the other side, too.

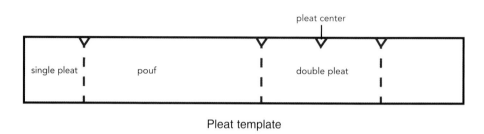

Pleat template

planning a balloon valance

A balloon valance consists of flat sections of fabric separated by pairs of pleats and framed at each edge by a single pleat. The standard pleat allowance is 12" (30 cm) for one pair of pleats and 6" (15 cm) for a single pleat. The pleat allowance can really be anywhere from 10" to 16" (26 to 41 cm)—whatever amount leaves enough room in between the pleats, on the flat sections, for your fabric motif. The flat sections are usually called "poufs," but they don't actually pouf until the pleats fall open when the valance is rigged.

Before they can be pleated to size for your window, almost all balloon valances need to be wider than the fabric width. So, you'll need to sew together two pieces of fabric to get the width you need. Instead of simply calculating the width needed (horizontal wall space + [pleat allowance x number of pleats]), you need to plan where the seams fall so they will be hidden inside a pleat. Here's what you do:

1. Decide how many poufs you want (an odd number looks best). To find the width of each pouf, divide the horizontal wall space by the number of poufs. In our sample, 51" wall space ÷ 3 poufs = 17" (129 cm ÷ 3 poufs = 43 cm).

2. See where the pleats fall. Make a sketch to help you visualize the pleats—it doesn't have to be in proportion. Draw a horizontal line. Mark a ½" (2 cm) seam allowance at one end, for joining the lining. Make a mark a short distance away from the first to represent 6" (15 cm) for the first pleat. Make another mark farther away to represent the first pouf. Write the dimension for the pouf width on your sketch (17" [43 cm] in our sample). Continue to mark all the poufs and pleats, ending with a single pleat and another ½" (2 cm) seam allowance. The sketch on the facing page shows the plan for the sample valance.

4 Lay the valance right side up on your work surface, with the top edge toward you. Align the template with the edge, placing the single-pleat space at the side edge. With pins or chalk, transfer the notch positions to the fabric. Move the template over and mark the next pouf space and double-pleat space.

5 Turn over the template and move it to mark the last pouf space and single-pleat space.

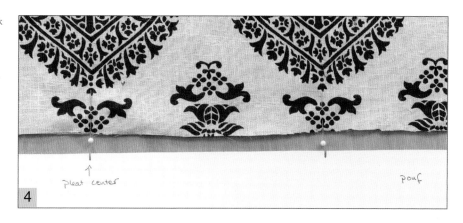

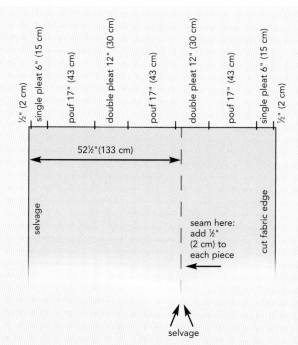

3. Add together the section dimensions to locate the position of the joining seam. Work with a calculator so you can easily see when the total approaches your fabric width. Begin at one end of your sketch and add the dimensions one at a time. Stop after you've added a pouf and before adding the next pleat that would make the total greater than the fabric width. On the sketch, you can see that the

marked span totals 52½" (133 cm). The next 12" (30 cm) pleat space would make the total span wider than our fabric, so the second fabric will be joined within that pleat space.

You can place the joining seam anywhere inside the pleat space except in the middle, where it would be most visible. The valance will look best if the seam is close to the pouf space. The seam will be hidden behind the pouf when the fabric is pleated. The fabric is 54" (138 cm) wide, so you'd use one full fabric width and then cut a second piece to fill out the remaining pleat and pouf spaces. (If the valance proportions were different or the fabric was another width, you might have to cut some width off both pieces of fabric in order to conceal the seam.)

When you plan the width for the second piece of fabric, don't forget to include a ½" (2 cm) seam allowance on each edge so you can sew the pieces together. If you like, you can cut and sew the fabric to be wider than you need overall and then cut it to size afterward.

balloon valance

6 To make the double pleats on the top edge, fold the fabric so that each mark indicating a pouf space edge aligns with the mark in the middle of the adjacent pleat space, as shown in the photo below. Pin the pleats through all layers, making sure the top edges align.

7 To make the single pleat at each end, fold the fabric so the mark closest to the end aligns with the side edge of the valance.

8 Sew across the top of each pleat with a ⅜" (1 cm) seam allowance and a long stitch.

9 To add the rod pocket, complete steps 10 through 14 of Pleated Tailored Valance on page 91.

10 To position the columns of rings that will control the draping, lay the valance flat, right side up, and fold the double pleats closed all the way to the bottom. Mark the middle of each set of pleats with a pin.

11 Turn the valance wrong side up and, with an L-square as a guide, draw a line perpendicular to the bottom at each pin mark.

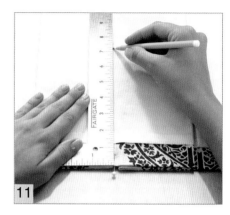

12 To indicate the placement for the rings, mark each drawn line ½" (1.5 cm) above the bottom edge and again at 7" (18 cm) intervals, making a total of three marks on each line. Mark the same intervals about ½" (1.5 cm) in from each side edge. Sew a ring at each mark and tie the rings together in columns (see the sidebar on page 53).

13 Slide the curtain rod into the rod pocket. If the rod has returns, make sure the inside of the rod is oriented toward the wrong side of the valance. Place the rod in its brackets or inside the window if it is a tension rod.

Want a more tailored look?
Pin the pleats closed at the bottom edge.
If you like the effect, sew them closed.

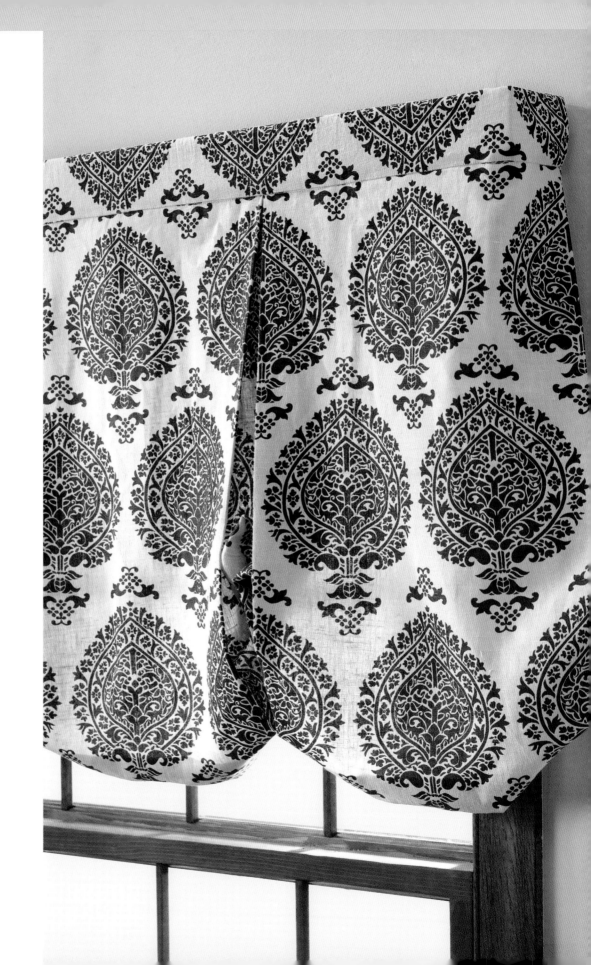

petticoat valance with covered cord

Work with complementary fabrics to make this pretty topper. It's made with two scalloped valances that are layered, offset by 2½" (6.5 cm), and pinned together at the top before sewing the rod pocket.

The Sample

- Shown with the top valance (A) in medium-weight floral-print cotton and the bottom valance (B) in cotton ticking. The ticking is cut on the bias for the cord.
- Fullness: 1½ times the horizontal wall space (including returns)
- Finished dimensions: 75" wide × 19" long (191 × 48 cm)

Supplies

- curtain rod (shown 2½" [6.5 cm] deep with 4½" [11.5 cm] returns)
- cable cord, enough to cover scalloped edge of valance plus 6" (15 cm)
- thread
- pins; scissors
- L-square and long straightedge
- pattern paper or muslin
- pressing templates: 4" (10 cm) and 3" (8 cm) deep (page 36)

Allowances

Top valance (A) face fabric

- Rod-pocket hem allowance (included in pattern, see step 1): 4" (10 cm)
- Bottom hem allowance (included in pattern, see step 1): ½" (2 cm)
- Joining seam allowance (if needed to join widths, add to each piece): ½" (2 cm)

- Side seam allowance (add to each vertical edge): ½" (2 cm)

Top valance lining

- Cut the lining the same size as the top valance face.

Bottom valance (B) face fabric and lining

- Cut the bottom valance fabrics the same width and 1½" (3.5 cm) shorter than the top fabrics.

Covered cord

- Cut enough 1¾" (4 cm)-wide bias strips to cover the scalloped edge of valance, plus 8" (21 cm) (page 32).

Measure, Plan, Buy Fabric

Determine the mounting style (page 14) and measure the window (page 25). Calculate your valance dimensions, basing the finished length on the desired distance from the top of the rod to the lower edge of the bottom valance. Refer to step 1 on page 100 and the cutting layout below to help you plan. Determine the yardage (page 29).

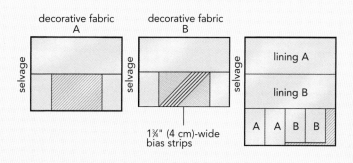

1 As explained on page 33, make a half-pattern for your valance. The length of the pattern, including allowances, should be the finished length from the top of the rod to the lower edge of the bottom valance (B), plus 2" (4 cm). Draw a line parallel to and 1½" (3.5 cm) below the top edge—this is the cutting line for the bottom valance (B). Refer to the diagrams below as you work. The first diagram shows the pattern. The second shows how the finished valances overlap. Set aside your pattern.

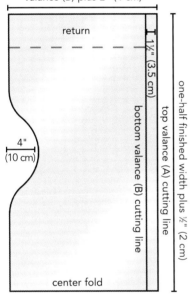

finished length from top of rod
to lower edge of bottom
valance (B) plus 2" (4 cm)

return

1½" (3.5 cm)

top valance (A) cutting line

bottom valance (B) cutting line

one-half finished width plus ½" (2 cm)

4"
(10 cm)

center fold

1" (2 cm)
turn-under

top valance

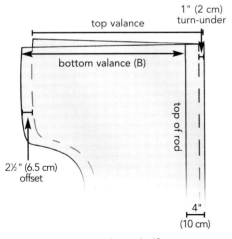

bottom valance (B)

top of rod

2½" (6.5 cm)
offset

4"
(10 cm)

Petticoat valance half-pattern

here's a hint!

If you're not sure how short you want the top valance to be, cut both valances so they are longer than you need. Sew each and test the overlap. Then cut off any excess, making sure to leave the rod-pocket hem allowance on the top valance.

2 Cut out the decorative fabric pieces for both layers of the valance, as described on page 99. Cut them to the greatest length needed, without shaping the lower edge. If you need to join two or more pieces of fabric to get the right width, sew them together. Press open the seam allowances. Also cut and join the pieces for the lining for both layers.

3 Fold the joined decorative fabric for valance A in half along its vertical center. Place your half-pattern on top, aligning the center fold, side, and top edges. Cut the bottom edge. Cut the lining in the same way.

4 Cut the bottom edge of the decorative fabric for valance B, making sure the line drawn on the pattern is even with the top edge of the fabric. You can fold the pattern on the line, if you wish. Cut the bottom edge of the lining, too.

5 Make the covered cord, as explained in the sidebar on the facing page.

6 Sew the covered cord to the bottom edge of the decorative fabric for valance B. Follow the directions in Attaching Decorator Cord on page 79. The fabric flange extending from the cord is equivalent to the tape on decorator cord. Because the flange is on the bias, it will easily stretch to follow the outside curve.

7 To sew the lining to the decorative fabric for each valance, follow steps 5, 6, and 7 of Pointed Valance with Cord-and-Tassel Trim on page 76. Disregard the reference to the tassel in step 6.

8 For valance A, work with the 4" (10 cm) and 3" (8 cm) templates to press a 3" (8 cm) single hem for the rod pocket (pages 37–38). Do not pin the hem.

9 Place valance A wrong side up on your work surface, with the pressed hem toward you. Unfold the hem. Place valance B wrong side up on top, aligning its top edge with the second fold from the cut edge of valance A, as shown in the photo below. Pin the layers together about 4" (10 cm) away from fold.

10 Fold the hem on A again, folding it over the top of B. Pin through all layers along the fold that's farthest away from you, as shown in the photo below. Remove the pins inserted in step 9.

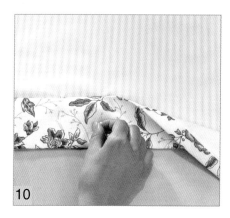

Try making one layer from lace!

11 Sew the rod pocket, stitching through all layers, close to the pinned fold.

12 Slide the curtain rod into the rod pocket. If the rod has returns, make sure the inside of the rod is oriented toward the wrong side of the valance. Place the rod in its brackets or inside the window if it is a tension rod.

making a covered cord

Fabric-covered cord is an inexpensive and easy-to-sew decorative accent. It is pretty and sophisticated, but not quite as fancy as fringe or braid. The filler cord is available in most fabric stores—either in small packages or by the yard.

1. First cut the fabric into bias strips (page 32). Lay the strips end-to-end in a straight line, wrong sides up. Pin the adjacent ends right sides together. Sew the strips together at the pins.

2. Press open the seam allowances. Then press the entire strip, stretching it gently.

3. Put the cording foot or zipper foot on the machine. Starting at one end, wrap the fabric around the cord, aligning the long edges of the fabric. You can pin the fabric around the cord to hold it in place, if you like. Sew close to the cord.

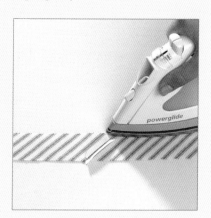

curtain panels with side borders

Here's a quick way to dress up a plain curtain panel. Just sew contrasting bands of fabric to the vertical edges of the panel. Then sew the lining to the free edges of the bands. No side hems required! Instead of sewing a rod pocket, hang the panels on a curtain pole with rings.

The Sample

- Shown in medium-weight printed silk with plain silk bands
- Fullness: 2 times the horizontal wall space
- Finished dimension of each panel: 48" wide × 86" long (123 × 218 cm)

Supplies

- curtain rod (decorative type with rings is shown)
- thread
- curtain weights (2 per panel)
- pins
- scissors
- L-square and long straightedge
- pressing template: 6" (16 cm) (page 36)

Allowances

Central panel

- Subtract 5" (12 cm) from the planned finished width to find the cut width (includes two ½" [2 cm] side seam allowances).
- Top allowance: ½" (2 cm)
- Bottom hem allowance: 6" (16 cm)
- Joining seam allowance (if needed to join widths, add to each piece): ½" (2 cm)

Top facing

- Cut one piece from the central panel fabric 4½" (13 cm) deep and the same width as the central panel.

Borders

- Cut two borders 7" (19 cm) wide and the same length as the central panel.

Lining

- Cut the lining the same width as and 5" (13 cm) shorter than the central panel.

Measure, Plan, Buy Fabric

Calculate your panel dimensions (the borders are included in the finished width) and determine the yardage (page 29). Include the allowances listed here in your dimensions. These cutting instructions are for only one panel. Refer to the cutting layout diagram at right to help you plan.

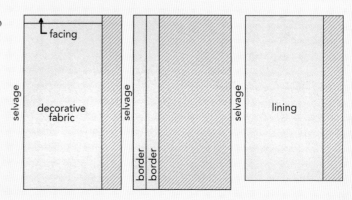

curtain panels with side borders

1 Cut out the fabric pieces for the central panel and facing, the borders, and the lining, as described on page 103. If you need to join two or more pieces of fabric to get the right width for the central panel, facing, or lining, sew them together with a ½" (2 cm) seam allowance. Press open the seam allowances. If you are making more than one panel, repeat this step for each panel. Do the same for all the rest of the steps, too.

2 Fold and press each band in half lengthwise, right side out.

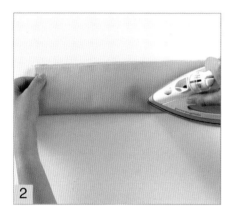

3 Unfold the bands. Pin and sew one long edge of one band to one vertical edge of the central panel, with right sides together. Pin and sew the other band to the opposite edge of the panel. Press open the seam allowances.

4 Working with the 6" (16 cm) template, press a double hem at the bottom of the joined panel and borders (page 36)—the finished hem will be 3" (8 cm) deep.

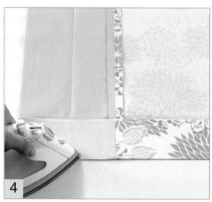

5 Pin the hem so it's ready to blindstitch by machine (page 38). Select the blindstitch setting on your machine and sew the hem. Hem the lining panel in the same way.

6 Pin the long edge of the top facing to the top of the lining panel, with right sides together. Sew the pieces together with a ½" (2 cm) seam allowance. Press the seam allowance toward the facing.

7 Matching the top corners, pin and sew the free long edge of one border to one vertical edge of the lining with a ½" (2 cm) seam allowance. Repeat to sew the other border to the opposite edge of the lining. The pieces now form a tube. Press the seams toward the borders.

adding curtain weights

To insert curtain weights, separate the decorator fabric and lining at the bottom corner of the curtain, unfolding the side facing. Place the seam allowance that has been pressed onto the facing under the presser foot. Lay the curtain weight on the facing, opposite the lining hem, placing the weight flange on the seam allowance. Sew the seam allowance and flange to the facing. Use a zipper foot if you like. When the facing and lining are folded against the curtain again, you'll see the line of stitching that secures the weight to the facing, as shown in the photo at far right.

8 Lay the panel (still inside out) flat on your work surface with the top edge closest to you and the borders at the sides. Gently fold the borders along the pressed creases so that the seams on both layers line up. Pin together the top edges.

9 Sew the pinned edges with a ½" (2 cm) seam allowance. Trim the allowance at the top corners. Turn the panel right side out. Press the top edge. If necessary, re-press the side creases.

10 At each bottom corner of the panel, sew a weight to the inside of the border (adjacent to the lining) to help the curtain hang evenly, as explained in the sidebar on the facing page.

11 Attach the decorative rings to the top of the panel at each end and evenly spaced across. To find the spacing interval, divide the panel width by a number that is one fewer than the number of rings (for seven rings, divide the panel width by 6). If your rings are the sew-on style, position the eyelet (the little ring at the bottom of the large decorative ring) on the wrong side of the curtain, just below the top edge of the fabric. The eyelet should not be visible when the curtain is hung.

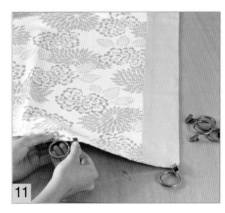

12 Slide the rings onto the curtain pole. Place the pole in its brackets, making sure that the curtain lining is toward the window.

Dress up solid fabrics
by adding tassel fringe
along the border seams.

tie-up curtain with band and cuff

The band at the top of this light and airy window treatment acts like a valance. The cuff—a fabric strip inserted between the band and draped skirt—adds a sweet accent.

The Sample

- Shown with medium-weight printed cotton for the band and lightweight linen for the skirt. The cuff and ties are made of taffeta.
- Fullness: 1 time the horizontal wall space (including returns), plus 1" (3 cm) for ease.
- Finished dimension: 52" wide by 58" long (132 cm × 148 cm); 27" (69 cm) long at shortest point when rigged.

Supplies

- curtain rod (shown 2½" [6.5 cm] deep with 4½" [11.5 cm] returns)
- thread
- 12 small plastic rings
- 1 yd. (1 m) shade cord, cut in half
- pins
- scissors
- L-square and long straightedge
- pressing templates: 6" (16 cm) and 3" (8 cm) deep (page 36)
- hand-sewing needle

Cutting List

Top band

- The finished band is 10" (26 cm) long. Cut it 1" (4 cm) wider than the finished width of your treatment and 16½" (44 cm) long. These dimensions include 6" (16 cm) for the rod-pocket hem allowance and a ½" (2 cm) seam allowance on all other edges.
- Cut one band and one same-size lining.

Inserted cuff and ties

- Cut one cuff to the same width as the band and 5" (14 cm) long.
- Cut 4 ties 5" wide × 37" long (14 × 98 cm).

Curtain skirt

- To find the finished length of the skirt, subtract 10" (26 cm) from the total finished length of your treatment.
- Top seam allowance: ½" (2 cm)
- Bottom hem allowance: 3" (8 cm)
- Joining seam allowance (if needed to join widths, add to each piece): ½" (2 cm)
- Side hem allowance: 3" (8 cm)

Measure, Plan, Buy Fabric

Determine the mounting style (page 14) and measure the window (page 25). Calculate your curtain dimensions, basing the total finished length on the distance from the top of the rod to windowsill. Figure the cut size of each piece, adding the allowances. Determine the yardage (page 29). If you railroad the fabric, as done for this project, use the cut width instead of the cut length to figure the yardage. Refer to the cutting layout on page 108 to help you plan.

1 | Cut out all the fabric pieces for the treatment. If you need to join two or more pieces of fabric to get the right width, sew them together with a ½" (2 cm) seam allowance. Press open the seam allowances.

2 | Press and sew mitered hems on the side and bottom edges of the curtain skirt, as explained in steps 2 through 6 of Cloud Valance on page 52.

3 | Fold each tie in half lengthwise, wrong side out. Sew the long edges together with a ½" (2 cm) seam allowance. Pivot and sew across one end. Trim the corner seam allowance at the sewn end. Gently poke the sewn end of the tie through to the open end with a small ruler to turn the ties right side out. Press.

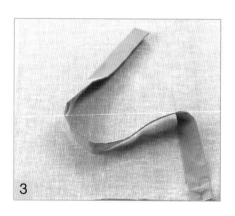

4 | Divide the width of the curtain skirt by 4. On the top edge of the skirt, measure and mark that distance from the side edges. Center the open end of a tie on each mark. Place the ties in pairs, one on the front and one on the back of the skirt.

5 | Fold the cuff in half lengthwise, wrong side out, and pin each end closed. Sew across each end with a ½" (2 cm) seam allowance. Turn the ends right side out and fold the cuff in half lengthwise again. Press the fold.

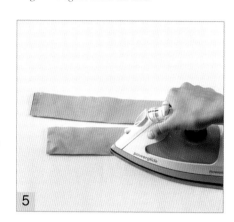

6 | Pin the cuff to the right side of the skirt, aligning the raw (top) edges. Sew together with a ⅜" (1 cm) seam allowance and a long stitch.

cutting layout

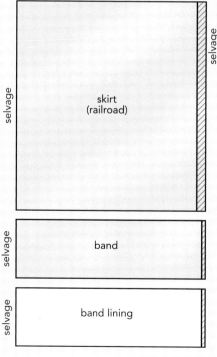

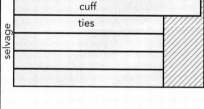

Note: This design should not have obvious vertical seams. If your desired finished width is wider than your fabric, railroad the pieces (page 31). If you cannot railroad the skirt, plan so the seams fall behind the ties.

7 Lay the band lining on your work surface, right side up, with the bottom edge toward you. Lay the skirt right side up on top, centering it so the band extends by ½" (2 cm) at each end and aligning the top of the skirt with the bottom of the band. Lay the decorative fabric band right side down on top, aligning it with the edges of the band lining as shown in the photo. Pin the top edge through all layers.

8 Sew the band and lining to the skirt as pinned, with a ½" (2 cm) seam allowance. Then pin the band and lining together at each end, being careful to tuck the skirt sandwiched between them out of the way. Sew each end as pinned, with a ½" (2 cm) seam allowance. You may want to attach the zipper foot.

9 Trim the seam allowance at the sewn corners. Pull the band up, turning it right side out. Press the seams, making sure both the lining and band face are smooth.

10 Press and then sew the rod pocket at the top of the band, as shown in the sidebar on page 45. Work with the 6" (16 cm) pressing template—the finished pocket will be 3" (8 cm) deep).

11 Sew the rings to the wrong side of the skirt, as shown in the sidebar on page 53. Make two columns with six rows of rings. Place the columns at the same distance from the side edge as the ties. Space the rows at 7" (18 cm) intervals, placing the first row just above the bottom edge. Tie the rings together, as shown in the sidebar.

12 Slide the curtain rod into the rod pocket. If the rod has returns, make sure the inside of the rod is oriented toward the wrong side of the curtain. Place the rod in its brackets or inside the window if it is a tension rod.

13 Tie a bow with each pair of ties, just below the draped skirt.

For a pretty finish on sheer fabric, embroider a decorative stitch on the right side of the hem.

Creative Publishing international

Copyright © 2008
Creative Publishing international, Inc.
400 First Avenue North, Suite 300
Minneapolis, MN 55401
1-800-328-3895
www.creativepub.com

ISBN-13: 978-1-58923-351-5
ISBN-10: 1-58923-351-4

10 9 8 7 6 5 4 3 2

Library of Congress
Cataloging-in-Publication Data
Easley, Madlyn.
  Quick and easy window treatments : 15 easy-
sew projects that build skills, too / Madlyn
Easley.
      p. cm. -- (Easy singer style)
  ISBN 1-58923-351-4
  1. Draperies. 2. Window shades. I. Title. II.
Series.
  TT390.E28 2008
  746.9'4--dc22   CIP
              007044022

Technical Editor: Carol Spier
Copy Editor: Iris Bass
Proofreader: Rebecca Silverman Fitzgerald
Book Design and Page Layout: Claire
MacMaster, barefoot art graphic design
Illustrations: Michael Wanke

Printed in China

acknowledgments

This book would not exist had I not been taught to sew by my
mother, Hattie Canders, who was a wonderful teacher. I started
sewing on her SINGER machine when I was seven years old. She
was very patient with me, but more important, she was a perfec-
tionist and would accept nothing less than straight seams and
neat finishing. Mom also instilled in me a love of fabric. One of
our favorite pastimes was shopping together to find just the right
material for whatever we were about to make. I'm fortunate that I
not only learned to sew, but, so much better, learned to do it
right and enjoy it.

Thanks to Deborah Cannarella for asking me to do this book and
to Carol Spier for figuring out how to make the information easy
to understand. The three of us had a wonderful time planning
the projects and selecting the perfect fabric for each. I hope you
will be inspired by our choices and enjoy planning and sewing
your own wonderful window treatments.

about the author

Madlyn Easley has been professionally designing window treat-
ments for more than twenty-five years. She and her company,
Athena Trading Company, have designed and manufactured
products for the Country Curtains and Spiegel catalogs, Soft
Surroundings, Bed, Bath & Beyond, Linens & Things, and Eddie
Bauer, and for many curtains shops. Madlyn holds three United
States patents for unique window treatment installation proce-
dures. She lives in Norwich, Connecticut.

suppliers

Fabric, Thread, and Notions
Calico Corners
800.213.6366
www.calicocorners.com

Hancock Fabrics, Inc.
877.322.7427
www.hancockfabrics.com

Jo-Ann Fabric and Craft Stores
888.739.4120
www.joann.com

Window Treatment Hardware
Bed Bath & Beyond, Inc.
800.462.3966
www.bedbathandbeyond.com

Sewing Machines and Accessories
SINGER Sewing Company
1224 Heil Quaker Boulevard
LaVergne, TN 37086
615.213.0880
www.singerco.com
SINGER sewing machines are available at authorized SINGER retailers.

Online Sources
Online sources for home décor fabrics
and window treatment hardware
include:

House Fabric
www.housefabric.com

Fabrics and Home
www.fabricsandhome.com

Interior Mall
www.interiormall.com

Fabricland
www.fabricland.com

Project Fabrics
Listed here by project are the fabrics
used in this book. They are available
from the listed wholesale sources
through an interior designer or from
some retail fabric vendors or home
décor workrooms.

Valance with Tucked Hem, page 42
Fabric: Polka; color: Orchard
Richloom Fabrics (212.685.7707)

Café Curtains with Heading, page 46
Fabric: Discontinued

Cloud Valance, page 50
Fabric: Adare; color: Celadon #27
Covington Fabrics (212.689.2200)

Simple Tie-up Curtain, page 54
Fabric: Trumpet Bel; color: Boysenberry
Robert Allen (800.333.3777)

Valance with Belt-Loop Tabs, page 58
Fabric: Carimba; color: Fiesta
Bravo Fabrics (212.532.8670)

*Lined Tie-up with Buttoned Ties,
page 64*
Fabric: PTU #1168; color: 1619
Portfolio Textiles (800.533.1010)

Ruffled Cloud Valance, page 68
Main fabric: Big Dahlia; color:
    Raspberry
Robert Allen (800.333.3777)
Ruffle fabric: #25206; color:
    Fuchsia #299
Duralee (631.273.8800)

Scalloped Valance with Trim, page 72
Fabric: Boardwalk; color: Kiwi
Roth & Tompkins Textiles
(203.857.4537)

*Pointed Valance with Cord-and-Tassel
Trim, page 76*
Fabric: Odette; color: Marigold
Bravo Fabrics (212.532.8670)

*Lined Panels with Tabs and Tiebacks,
page 80*
Fabric: Flores; color: #19
Duralee (631.273.8800)

Pleated Tailored Valance, page 88
Fabric: Geotype; color: Brick
Robert Allen (800.333.3777)

Balloon Valance, page 92
Fabric: Ottoman CM-05178; color: #2
Noveltex (213.745.9999)

*Petticoat Valance with Covered Cord,
page 98*
Top Layer Fabric: Carmen #1124;
    color: #2
Noveltex (213.745.9999)
Bottom Layer Fabric: Ticking;
    color: #36
Covington Fabrics (212.689.2200)

*Curtain Panels with Side Borders,
page 102*
Main Fabric: Grace SH66;
    color: Jelly Bean
Border Fabric: Shantung SH66;
    color: Citron
Chris Stone (323.583.9957)

*Tie-up Valance with Band and Cuff,
page 106*
Top Band Fabric: #25202; color: #72
Duralee (631.273.8800)
Skirt Fabric: White Linen; color:
    Marseille 4A11206
Noveltex (213.745.9999)
Cuff fabric: Topaz; color: Powder
Fabricut (918.622.7700)

index